P9-DDZ-656

MISSIONARY MOVEMENT
OF THE NON-WESTERN CHURCHES

COMPENDIUM of 2010 EAST-WEST MISSION FORUM

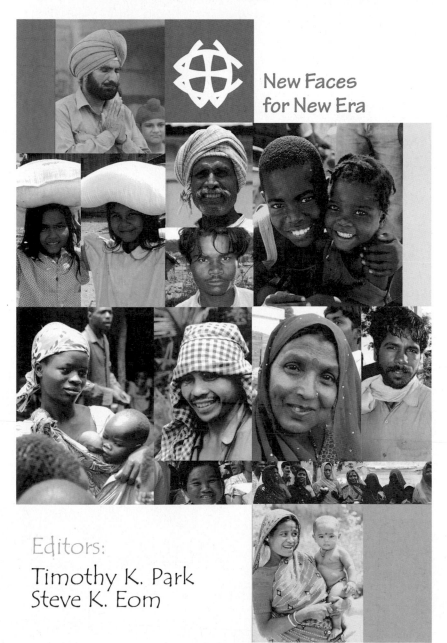

New Faces
for New Era

Editors:
Timothy K. Park
Steve K. Eom

MISSIONARY MOVEMENT OF THE NON-WESTERN CHURCHES

COMPENDIUM of
2010 EAST-WEST MISSION FORUM

Edited by

Timothy K. Park
Steve K. Eom

**EAST-WEST CENTER FOR
MISSIONS RESEARCH & DEVELOPMENT**

Published by
East-West Center for Missions Research & Development
464 E Walnut St, Suite 220
Pasadena, CA 91101
1-626-577-5564

ISBN:
978-89-965514-8-5 93230

$10.00

gratis

123996

2010 East-West Mission Forum Schedule

	7(Fri)	8(Sat)	9(Sun)	10(Mon)
8:00-8:30		Devotion I		Devotion II
8:30-10:00 (90min)		African Missionary Movement Dr. Seth Anyomi	Attending Sunday Worship Service	
10:00-10:30 (30min)		Break		
10:30-12:00 (90min)		Latin American Missionary Movement Decio de Carvalho		
12:00-1:30		Lunch		
1:30-3:00 (90min)		Asian Missionary Movement Dr. Timothy Park		Culture Tour
3:00-4:15 (75min)	Opening Service Welcome Address Dr. Chong Young Yee Keynote Speech: Trends of World Missionary Movement Dr. Jehu J. Hanciles	Break 3:00-3:30 Partnership in Missions Research and Development Dr. Dave Datema	David Cho Museum & Library Visit David Cho's Pilgrimage in Mission Dr. Eun Moo Lee	
4:15-4:30 (15min)	Break	3:30-5:00		
4:30-6:00 (90min)	Western Missionary Movement Dr. Paul Pierson	Break 5:00-6:00		
6:00-7:30	Dinner	Dinner		
7:30-9:00 (90 min)	Non-Western Missionary Movement Dr. David Cho	Retrospect and Prospect of EWC/mrd Dr. Yong Cho Round Table Talk: East-West Collaboration for Mission Research and Development Dr. David Hartono	Open Air Garden Banquet Host: GMS	Korean Cultural Presentation

TABLE OF CONTENTS

PREFACE

In the past, the missionary movement of the Christian church was predominantly led by the Western churches. In the 21st century, however, it has evolved to become a multi-ethnic, interdenominational, and international movement. Churches in Asia, Africa, and Latin-America have emerged as new missionary forces and are actively involved in the missionary movement. It is true that the Western church has ignored the non-western churches and non-western churches have devaluated western mission. Both must avoid a one-way mission mindset and pursue a partnership to accomplish the remaining task of world evangelization. In order to do this, we need to understand what God has been doing through other ethnic churches in other continents.

In celebrating the first anniversary of the David Cho Mission Museum and Library, established in 2009 for the purpose of research in Non-Western mission, the East-West Center for Missions Research & Development and the David Cho Missiological Institute joined forces to host the '2010 East-West Mission Forum' on May 7th-10th, 2010, at Mayfield Hotel and Hansarang Church in Gimpo, Korea. Missiologists, missions leaders, missions professors, and missionaries were invited to the forum and key missions leaders of each continents spoke on the world missionary movement, non-western missionary movement, Latin-American missionary movement, African missionary movement and Asian missionary movement.

The lineup of speakers for this forum represented the wide-spectrum of missions, both in the academic and research sector, as well as in the actual mission field. Dr. Jehu Hanciles of Fuller Graduate School of Intercultural Studies spoke on the Trends of World Missionary Movement, Dr. Paul E. Pierson on the Western Missionary Movement, Dr. David J. Cho on the Non-Western Missionary Movement, Dr. Seth Anyomi of African Christian Mission on the African Missionary Movement, Dr. Decio de Cavalho of COMIBAM on Latin-American Missionary Movement, and I on the Asian Missionary Movement. Reverend Dave Datema of US Center for World Mission spoke on Partnership in Missions Research and Development on behalf of Western Church, and Dr. Yong Cho spoke on the East-West Center for Missions Research and Development. Dr. Eunmoo Lee spoke on Dr. David Cho's Life and Ministry.

I am grateful to them for making excellent presentations. I hope this book will help readers understand what God has done in every continent through His people and help us recognize one another and pursue a better partnership in kingdom ministry.

Timothy K. Park, Ph.D.

President,
East-West Center for Missions Research & Development

TRENDS OF
WORLD MISSIONARY MOVEMENT

"We Have This Treasure in Earthen Vessels":
New Trends and Trajectories
in the Global Missionary Movement

Dr. Jehu J. Hanciles
Fuller Theological Seminary

TRENDS OF
WORLD MISSIONARY MOVEMENT

"We Have This Treasure in Earthen Vessels":
New Trends and Trajectories
in the Global Missionary Movement

It is now well known that Christianity's rate of expansion over the last 100 years exceeds any other period in its 2000-year history; and, significantly, much of this growth has taken place in parts of the world where Christian presence or representation was marginal to start with. The same period witnessed a dramatic erosion of Christian faith and presence in the Western world, hitherto the standard bearer of the faith. Of the 10 countries with the fastest growth between 1910 and 2010, six are in Africa and four in Asia.[1] By the closing decades of the twentieth century Africa and Latin America had emerged as the new heartlands of the faith. As such, the globalization of Christianity has led not to the worldwide dominance of Western Christendom but to the *re-emergence of Christianity as a non-Western religion*.

New Trends:
The Non-Western Missionary Phenomenon

This historic transformation within global Christianity has also been accompanied by—or at least drawn attention to—large scale, sustained, non-Western missionary initiatives that are international in scope and include forms of outreach

---

1. "World Christianity, 1910-2010," International Bulletin of Missionary Research 34, 1 (January, 2010).

into western societies. It is increasingly obvious that missionary initiatives from the churches in Asia, Africa, and Latin America have emerged as "the cutting edge of the Christian world mission".[2] This "global south missionary phenomenon" (as it is sometimes called) is only now beginning to draw scholarly attention. At least three factors must be taken into account in assessing its potential.

First, the reemergence of Christianity as a non-Western religion means that the face of global Christianity is now largely defined by economic poverty, daily hardships, and political weaknesses. In economic terms, the church in the non-Western world, taken as a whole, is not in a position to replicate key forms and practices associated with the Western missionary movement—including the missionary society approach and the specialist missionary model. Second, that the missionary impulse now so strongly evident within non-Western Christianities is not a novel development. It reflects a dynamism and vision that was present within non-Western Christianities long before the "shift" itself. The vast majority of African, Asian and Latin American Christians have heard the message of the gospel not from a foreign missionary but from compatriots or indigenous agents. Third, that the Western missionary movement, for all its glaring shortcomings, played a critical role in the establishment of Christianity in much of the non-Western world. While it was never as dominant as often depicted, the Western missionary movement epitomized the ideal of cross-cultural missionary engagement (enshrined in the gospel) in a way that is now part of a narrative that non-Western Christians can draw inspiration from in their own efforts.

In the final analysis, there can be little doubt that the global missionary landscape had changed dramatically by the end of the twentieth century. Mapping its contours and patterns is a different thing altogether.

---

2. Wilbert R. Shenk, "Recasting Theology of Mission: Impulses from the Non-Western World," ibid.25, 3 (July, 2001), 98.

New Trajectories in Christian Missions:
The Limits of Traditional Models and Measurements

On paper at least, the general contours and trend of the Christian missionary movement worldwide—in terms of formal sending across national boundaries—are clear enough: the numbers of missionaries from Europe and North America remain dominant but are steadily declining, while the number of foreign missionaries "officially sent" by churches in non-Western countries is increasing at an extraordinary rate. Yet even this seemingly straightforward picture is clouded by any number of complexities. Within the Western missionary movement, for instance, the prominent eruption of short term missions—perhaps involving more than 1½ million American Christians alone every year—and the dramatic rise in the number of non-Western missionaries supported by North American Protestant missionary agencies are worth mentioning.[3] In the case of the non-Western missionary movement, the challenges of assessment are greatly multiplied, in part because so much of it is clandestine, informal and unstructured (in most parts of the non-Western world cross-cultural missionary engagement does not require one to live one's country).

The complexity and multiplicity of the new missionary initiatives emerging out of the non-Western world defy straightforward analysis. To the limitations of statistical assessment must also be added major conceptual obstacles. Nonetheless, the extraordinary rise in non-Western missionary enterprise over the last three decades is inescapable.

A few individual examples from Africa, Asia and Latin America must suffice. One of the best examples of international Christian expansion from Africa is provided by the Ghana-based Church of Pentecost. Established in 1937 as a hugely grassroots movement, Church of Pentecost has grown into the largest Protestant church in Ghana, with

---

3. See Michael Jaffarian, "The Statistical State of the North American Protestant Missions Movement, from the Mission Handbook, 20th Edition," ibid.32, 1 (January, 2008), 37.

over 800,000 adult members in 2002. From the mid-1980s, Church of Pentecost assemblies (as its individual churches are called) have proliferated throughout Africa and beyond, in the Middle East, Europe, and North America. According to its website,[4] the number of assemblies established outside Ghana grew from 1,763 in 2004 to 2,905 in 2009—a 65 percent increase in five years. An official report states that "besides opening 180 foreign assemblies, 9,170 converts were baptised in the missions fields" in 2009 alone.[5] The Church has branches in some 75 countries on all the continents with as many officially commissioned individual missionaries.

By one account there were some 67,000 Asian missionaries by 2000.[6] The majority of officially funded missionaries are South Korean. South Korea sends a greater number of missionaries per Christian population than even the United States.[7] The Korean international missionary force exploded in numbers from around 500 in the mid-1980s to 14,086 (serving in 180 countries) by 2006.[8] Significantly, almost half (6,646 or 47.4%) were sent by denominational churches, while the rest (7,366 or 52.6%) came from parachurch mission agencies.

Latin Americans, writes Sergio Ramos, "have become one of the fastest-growing missionary movements around the world", with Latino missionaries serving in Africa, Middle East, Europe and other Latin American countries.[9]

4. http://thecophq.org/. See also Opoku Onyinah, "Pentecostalism and the African Diaspora: An Examination of the Missions Activities of the Church of Pentecost," Pneuma 26, 2 (Fall, 2004), 229.

5. S. K. Amegah, Pentecost Chalks Success (Church of Pentecost, 2010).

6. Julie Ma, "The Growth of Christianity in Asia and Its Impact on Mission," Encounters Mission Ezine (16, 2007)3.

7. Todd M. Johnson, Kenneth R. Ross, and Sandra S. K. Lee, Atlas of Global Christianity 1910-2010 (Edinburgh: Edinburgh University Press, 2009), 259.

8. Timothy Kiho Park, "Korean Christian World Mission: The Missionary Movement of the Korean Church," in Missions from the Majority World: Progress, Challenges, and Case Studies, ed. Enoch Wan and Michael Pocock (Pasadena, CA: William Carey Library, 2009), 98. Perhaps as high as 19,000 according to unofficial sources—cf. www.kidok.com.

9. Sergio A. Ramos, "Hispanic/Latino Oppurtunities for Sharing the Love

Undoubtedly, the most significant missionary initiative out of Latin America in terms of formal structure is COMIBAM (*Cooperación Misionera Ibero-Americana*)—an "indigenous interdenominational network concerned with world missions from Latin America" established in 1987.[10] Largely due to its efforts, Protestant missionaries sent from Latin America to other parts of the world had mushroomed from an estimated 1,600 Protestant missionaries (from 70 agencies) in 1987 to 10,000 missionaries (from about 400 organizations) by 2006. Some 17 percent of these serve in Europe; second only to the proportion (36 percent) serving in South America.

These structured non-Western missionary efforts are not without shortcomings, including limited missionary training, unquestioning imitation of traditional Western models, and overdependence on financial support from Western churches or agencies. But they also possesses major strengths. The missionaries often enjoy access (without visa restrictions) to countries in their regions that are closed to Western missionaries. Their ability to live on the same economic level as the people among whom they live and minister also places a lower financial burden on sending churches or mission organizations. This, combined with the added advantage of cultural affinity with the peoples among whom they work—as in the case of Latinos within Arab culture[11]—potentially translates into more effective outreach.

Migration and Mission

But formal or structured missionary initiatives involving non-Western missionary agencies represents little more than the tip of the iceberg, so to speak, of the emerging non-

of Jesus with Muslims," ibid., ed. Enoch Wan and Michael Pocock (Pasadena, CA: William Carey Library, 2009), 265.

10. Julio Guarneri, "Comiban: Calling Latin Americans to the Global Challenge," ibid., ed. Enoch Wan and Michael Pocock (Pasadena, CA: William Carey Library, 2009), 227; also, Samuel Escobar, Changing Tides: Latin America and World Mission Today (Maryknoll, NY: Orbis Books, 2002), 159f.

11. Ramos, "Hispanic/Latino Oppurtunities for Sharing the Love of Jesus with Muslims," , 267.

Western missionary phenomenon. A substantial dimension of the phenomenon is embedded in global migratory flows. So much so that inattentiveness to the strong links between human migration and religious expansion will greatly impair any meaningful assessment of new trends and trajectories within the global missionary movement. The integral role of migration is one prominent reason why the new non-Western missionary movement is of a scale and magnitude that defy empirical assessment. Much more than the older and still significant Western missionary project, the nature and trajectory of the non-Western missionary movement is greatly defined by human mobility.

Even as I write this, millions of non-Western Christian migrants are fulfilling a "missionary" function within their own countries or continents and beyond. This is because, from a biblical point of view, every Christian migrant is a potential missionary. Since the 1960s, the vast majority of international migrants have come from the non-Western world and the main destination countries include the European nations that had been the main source of international migrants in previous centuries. Many are also included in the new wave of migrants that have been drawn to the wealthy oil producing states in the Middle East.[12] In effect, the nature and direction of global migratory flows are such that untold numbers of non-Western Christian migrants have found themselves in different parts of the world where a good many have been thrust into missionary action.

The growing presence of burgeoning non-Western immigrant populations in Western societies is a matter of record. The point is that among the swelling tide of guest workers, students, labor migrants, asylum seekers, political and economic refugees that constitute the world's migrant population are numerous Christians—each one a potential missionary. In Europe, where the immigration debates focus mainly on Muslim populations, the significance of Christian

---

12. By the early 1990s, foreign workers in these oil rich states (mainly from Africa and Asia) numbered over 7 million—W. M. Spellman, The Global Community: Migration and the Making of the Modern World (Stroud, England: Sutton Publishing, 2002)163.

migrants is typically overlooked. In the USA, where the majority of new immigrants are Christian, the focus on illegal immigration often precludes awareness that immigration is rapidly transforming the Christian landscape—for instance, a third of all American Roman Catholics are now Hispanic. In the Middle East also, thousands of household Filipino maids (many Christian) are entrusted with the welfare and oversight of children in affluent Arab families[13]—with at least notional missionary possibilities.

The Non-Western Missionary Movement and Western Society

The unprecedented scale and volume of post-1960s South-to-North migratory flows clearly portend long term transformations of Western societies. Within a few decades, Christian immigrants have established flourishing congregations in Western countries that represent the main centers of Christian growth and vitality. While their strong missionary outlook is well attested questions persist about their potential missionary impact. The matter is complex. Undoubtedly, the prospects for successful cross-cultural outreach are daunting: serious challenges are posed by racial rejection, social marginalization, aggressive secularism and, sadly, self-inflicted wounds. Yet, the "new mission churches" (as they are sometimes called in Europe) represent the face of Christianity to untold numbers of the non-/ no longer Christian and their missionary effectiveness will arguably increase with acculturation and naturalization. In the American context, the churches that demonstrate the strongest missionary vitality and the most robust growth are undoubtedly the new immigrant churches or ethnic congregations established within various denominations.

Attuned to an ideal of the "missionary" as a trained individual sent to a foreign territory by a self-designated missionary body, many Western observers are liable to dismiss the potential impact of these new initiatives/

13. Enoch Wan and Michael Pocock, Missions from the Majority World: Progress, Challenges, and Case Studies, vol. no. 17 (Pasadena, CA: William Carey Library, 2009), 401.

movements too quickly. Yet an exclusive dependence on Western models and conceptualizations greatly impairs our ability to understand the new realities and fully explore the "new world Christian movement". To start with, the new heartlands of the faith in the non-West are radically different in character and function from the preceding heartlands in the West. The latter was marked to a significant extent by economic power, territorial domination, national religion, and cultural superiority; in acute contrast, the emerging heartlands of the faith are marked by poverty and suffering, religious plurality, immense diversity of Christian experience and expression, and structures of dependency. Even with the emergence of a few Asian nations as global economic powers, the vast majority of people who form the non-Western missionary movement act from a position of powerlessness, weakness, and hardship. This is strongly reflected in the movement's entrenched linkage to global migratory flows.

Empirical assessment of a phenomenon as dynamic and organic as missionary movement and action will always be subject to profound limitations. The common evangelical assumption that we can tell what God is doing in the world by means of empirical measurements or statistical assessment is untenable. In any case, the new trends within the global missionary movement are shaped by unprecedented developments and unique elements that call for fresh assessments. The new world Christian missionary movement is marked by multitudinous initiatives and disparate movements that are framed by fluid structures and unofficial activities of great variety and complexity. The predominance of migrant movement is striking; not least because the migrants epitomize disempowerment, marginalization, and loss of status. In this regard, the biblical reference to "treasure in earthen vessels" is palpably relevant. It provides a vital reminder that while the Christian missionary enterprise may reflect human agency, ingenuity and planning it is ultimately God's church and God's mission. And He specializes in using the weak things of the world.

Bibliography

Amegah, S. K. *Pentecost Chalks Success*. Church of Pentecost, 2010.

Escobar, Samuel. *Changing Tides: Latin America and World Mission Today.* American Society of Missiology Series No. 31, ed. Escobar Samuel. Maryknoll, NY: Orbis Books, 2002.

Guarneri, Julio. "Comiban: Calling Latin Americans to the Global Challenge." In *Missions from the Majority World: Progress, Challenges, and Case Studies*, ed. Enoch Wan and Michael Pocock, no. 17, 221-62. Pasadena, CA: William Carey Library, 2009.
9788097808099

Jaffarian, Michael. "The Statistical State of the North American Protestant Missions Movement, from the *Mission Handbook*, 20th Edition." *International Bulletin of Missionary Research* 32, no. 1 (January, 2008): 35-38.

Johnson, Todd M., Kenneth R. Ross, and Sandra S. K. Lee. *Atlas of Global Christianity 1910-2010*. Edinburgh: Edinburgh University Press, 2009.

Ma, Julie. "The Growth of Christianity in Asia and Its Impact on Mission." *Encounters Mission Ezine*, no. 16 (2007).

Onyinah, Opoku. "Pentecostalism and the African Diaspora: An Examination of the Missions Activities of the Church of Pentecost." *Pneuma* 26, no. 2 (Fall, 2004): 216-41.

Park, Timothy Kiho. "Korean Christian World Mission: The Missionary Movement of the Korean Church." In *Missions from the Majority World: Progress, Challenges, and Case Studies*, ed. Enoch Wan and

Michael Pocock, no. 17, 97-120. Pasadena, CA: William Carey Library, 2009.

Ramos, Sergio A. "Hispanic/Latino Oppurtunities for Sharing the Love of Jesus with Muslims." In *Missions from the Majority World: Progress, Challenges, and Case Studies*, ed. Enoch Wan and Michael Pocock, no. 17, 263-81. Pasadena, CA: William Carey Library, 2009.

Shenk, Wilbert R. "Recasting Theology of Mission: Impulses from the Non-Western World." *International Bulletin of Missionary Research* 25, no. 3 (July, 2001): 98-107.

Spellman, W. M. *The Global Community: Migration and the Making of the Modern World*. Stroud, England: Sutton Publishing, 2002.

Wan, Enoch, and Michael Pocock. *Missions from the Majority World: Progress, Challenges, and Case Studies*. Vol. no. 17 Evangelical Missiological Society Series. Pasadena, CA: William Carey Library, 2009.

"World Christianity, 1910-2010." *International Bulletin of Missionary Research* 34, no. 1 (January, 2010): 32-33.

WESTERN MISSIONARY MOVEMENT

History, Current Issues and Trends in the Global Missionary Movement

Dr. Paul Pierson
Fuller Theological Seminary

East-West
Mission Forum

WESTERN MISSIONARY
MOVEMENT

History, Current Issues and Trends
in the Global Missionary Movement

I. The missionary movement began in the 18th century, as the result of renewal movements which sought to move beyond the Christendom model in Europe and its nominalism. E.g, Pietism, Moravians, Evangelical awakenings.

In general, it was not supported by the established churches at the beginning. E.G. Carey, LMS, CMS, others. In United States, the ABCFM, the Baptists.

I. The Assumptions

A. First Assumption: Wholistic, The sharing of the Gospel and the growth of the Church would bring social progress. James Dennis; Christian Missions and Social Reform. Too optimistic.

B. Second assumption: Western Christianity was the norm. Churches in other nations should look like those in the West.

C. Third assumption: Western culture was Christian. The Christian life in other nations should look like that in the West.

D. Fourth assumption; Western theology was the norm. It did not deal with many issues in non-western cultures; for example, the ancestors and spirits. The miraculous. How to deal with poverty and political oppression, how to relate to western colonialism.

E. Fifth assumption (at first) leadership in the hands of western missionaries, in most but not all cases. Korea, Brazil were exceptions.

III. We must recognize the amazing heroism and sacrifice of many. The great numbers who died. Judson's two wives as examples. In Africa, often half were dead within six months.

IV. The Accomplishments

A. Churches were established in many nations. Wm Temple in 1942. "The Great New Fact of our Time." The church exists in nearly every nation on earth. There were probably five exceptions, Nepal one of them.

B. Schools and universities were established. This often opened education to girls and women and the poor. Examples; MacKenzie University in Sao Paulo. Ehwa University in Seoul. Speaking of the women's missionary movement, Beaver called it the "first feminist movement in North America," and added that it "set in motion forces that still work for the liberation of women in Asia and Africa."

C. Modern medicine introduced, hospitals, clinics, medical and nursing schools. Treatment of lepers and tuberculosis. Dr. Ida Scudder and the great medical center at Vellore, India, is an example.

D. In a number of cases, new agricultural methods were introduced. Dr. Sam Higgenbottom and the agricultural college at Allahabad, India.

V. The end of Concensus at the beginning of the 20th century

A. The Fundamentalist/Modernist struggle. Mission as social reform or mission as saving souls.

B. The attitude toward other religions. The Hocking

Report, 1932. Seek the best in all religions. The reaction by Kraemer, Speer, others."The Finality of Jesus Christ."

VI. The Edinburgh Conference, 1910

A. Inclusive; High Anglicans to Faith Missions, e.g. China Inland Mission.
B. 1200 delegates, all from the West except for 17 Asians.
C. Focus on cooperation. Led to formation of the International Missionary Council.
D. Understanding of mission; from 'Christian countries' to 'non-Christian countries.' Still assumed the West was Christian. Christendom concept.

VII. From 1945 to 2010

A. From optimism (1945) to great pessimism (1949). China, Communism, the end of colonialism.
B. The decline of 'mainline' denominational missions; from 60% of North American mission personnel in 1935 to 5% or less today. The growth of Evangelical, Charismatic, and independent missions, mainly multidenominational, today. It is important to examine the reasons for decline in these historic groups. I believe the reasons are twofold; one is theological 'erosion,' the loss of the centrality of the Gospel; the other is the loss of focused mission structures, for example, the move in my denomination from a Board of Foreign Missions to a Program Agency.
C. We see two kinds of ecumenism today, both having roots in the missionary movement.

   a. The first is the World Council of Churches. The International Missionary Council became part of the WCC in 1961. While the original hope was that unity would lead to more mission, the opposite has been the case. Mission in the sense of the communication of the Gospel to non-Christians, does not seem to be an important part of the agenda of the WCC.

b. The other is the new evangelical ecumenism. It has been centered in the Lausanne Movement, Its covenant adopted in 1974, is one of the great Christian documents of the 20th century. The 1982 document, 'Evangelism and Social Responsibility, is also important. Another result of Lausanne, 1974, was the change in focus in mission from geography to culture. Ralph Winter's address on 'unreached peoples' was an epoch making event.

VIII. Some of the Issues to be faced in our Changing Era

A. The importance of growing discipleship, a deeper understanding of the Christian life; focused inward on the person (union with Christ), on the Christian community, and outward toward the world. A theology of the Kingdom of God.

B. Globalization and Migration. Mission is now from everywhere to everywhere. E.g. Magdy, an Egyptian Christian evangelizing Muslims in an American university community.

C. Urbanization. The need for new forms of the Church. Incarnational ministry among the urban poor.

D. Transformation; Evangelism and Development. AIDS.

E. Contextualization and 'Insider Movements.'

F. The need for partnerships and greater cooperation.

G. The need for new methods of leadership selection and training in the contexts of ministry.

NON-WESTERN MISSIONARY MOVEMENT

Perspectives on East-West Collaboration for Non-Western Mission Advance

Dr. David J. Cho
David Cho Missilogical Institute

NON-WESTERN MISSIONARY MOVEMENT

Perspectives on East-West Collaboration for Non-Western Mission Advance

PROLOGUE

I have requested Dr. Timothy Park to omit my name from the list of speakers of this forum. I also asked him to find someone who researched non-Western mission history. He, however, refused my request and insisted me to prepare a paper on 'Non-Western Mission History.'

Today, I am standing here on this platform because of Dr. Timothy Park's denial to my request. I want to share with all of you about my God's given special calling and my 60 years of history for the East-West cooperation for Non-Western missions advance and the progress of networking of Non-Western mission.

I. Who are We: The Third World or Non-Western World

The term Non-Western world was coined as the Third World by the Western mission leaders since 1960. I'd like to share with everyone who are the Third World. The Third World has a different world view from the Western view of the world. The Third World means the world which has lived a dark and shadowed life in the Eurocentric Age of the World.

A. Politically, Third World means the non-allied world. The nations that do not belong to the Eastern block or the Western block politically.

B. Economically, the Third World means the underdeveloped or developing countries which are suffering from poor economies because of the lack of management ability, and lack of development or international trade, in spite of their abundant natural resources.

C. Historically, the Third World were the colonial societies of the Western World.

D. Psychologically, the Third World wants to terminate from the remaining forces of the post-colonial society of the traditional imperialistic powers.

E. Racially or nationally, the Third World are the nations which fought for or gained their independence after World War II; nevertheless they are still fighting against chaos or disorder as they build their own nations.

F. Culturally the Third World means non-Western Culture.

G. Religiously, the Third World means the non-Christian world. In mission the Third World means the new forces of sending missions from countries which traditionally only received missionaries from Western Christendom.

H. Regionally, the Third World seems to belong to the "South". The Third World occupies 70% of the world land base. The Third World includes 77% of the world population. The Third World also means those who have lost their self-identity, those who have a high illiteracy rate, a low employment rate, a gulf between the rich and the poor, underdeveloped health services, high mortality rate, the co-existence of the modern and the primitive, and suffering from unceasing wars and battles waged for or by the superpowers.

I. On the other hand, the Third World is also the world with better preserved natural environments, with less pollution from modern sciences, with less of the decadent trend of modernism, and with more humane societies.

II. Distinction of Non-Western Missions from Traditional Western Missions

A. The Protestant mission of Western Christendom was originated in the colonial age of Western Christendom since AD 1790.

- It was Mission from Western Christendom to their colonies in Africa, with colonization of Asian nations.
- The Colonial mission coexisted with colonial power's conquest, ruling, and exploiting, and all of these were mingled together with mission.
- Mission was subverted by substituting Westernization for Christianization.
- Mission was the denominational expansion of Western Christendom instead of the planting of a national church.
- The peculiarity of Colonial mission was this mixture of Colony, Commerce and Christianity together.

B. Non-Western Missions were sprung up from the de-colonized Asian and African continents after the end of the Second World War, 1945. Most of them were the colonies of Western Christendom.

Since they were exploited and oppressed by the authorities of colonial powers, the de-colonized newly independent countries restricted missionary activities.
Under the unfavorable restricting Christian activities of ruling powers of one's own nation, the Asian church and African church were regenerated as the Christianity of their own nations from their former status transplanted denominational church of Western church.

By the divine providence, they began to be aware of the calling for missionary outreach beyond their own culture. They were exploited and oppressed for a long time as the colonies of Western Christendom and they were still poor and some of them were stateless people as refugees to the other continents. However, they did not stop the proclamation of the Gospel to the other people. This symptom was very much similar to the Apostolic mission in AD 30 to 100.

- Genes of the Apostolic Mission were carried by the homeless, stateless and poorest of scattered refugees.
- Apostolic Mission was passed from oppressed powerless nations to wealthy powerful nations and a ruling superpower empire.
- Apostolic Mission was Itinerating Mission, crossing in all the directions of every culture.
- The center of Apostolic Mission was the eschatological mission which proclaims the Second Coming of Jesus.
- The Apostolic Mission survived martyrdom.

C. Currently, the differences of the world between West and East, between North and South are disappearing. They had to work separately in those days. It was difficult to create a common structure for working together. And we could leave all the work to the "have's" and the stronger people.

   But now it is impossible to have vertical or subordinate relationships among races and nations. Now we are "workers of the sunset" called for the last harvest in our global village, this last age requires a mutual approach and coexistence in which East and West are side by side. North and South are front to back. We have to work shoulder to shoulder and hand in hand. We cannot delay any longer. We should not stay outside the vineyard. The end of the world is approaching. We have to call the last mission forces without holding back any reserves.

   The movement of the Non-Western Missions Advance represents a promise not to step back from the biblical principles by which God only will be glorified and the Name of Jesus Christ be lifted on high. In this last age, filled with non-biblical Christian movements, wherein the stronger are the oppressors and the weaker are oppressed one and in which that divide themselves one from another for their own benefit.

   Because all races, nations and countries, whether big or small, whether rich or poor, whether strong or weak, are called from their natural place to minister within the Kingdom of God no one should use any humanitarian prejudice or denominational ambition, or any traditional Christian system or structure, to hinder or oppress our independent, indigenous and spontaneous efforts.

As the world is divided into many ideologies, cultures and social structures, we must recognize and respect the fact that we think differently and our situations are different from one another. But at the same time, because we know that the One God called us and commands us, we have to understand one another, respect one another, share one another's burden and accomplish our common goals by sharing resources with the weaker, the poorer, the less powerful among us to meet each others' needs. Indeed our united action for Non-Western Missions Advance is a new movement. We represent new forces. It is unwise to put new wine into old wineskins. I have been making a new wineskin to hold new wine.

To speak about a new age and a new world means new times and new places replacing an the old age and old world, from the age of Mediterranean nations, the 16th Century, and the finding of a new world. The 19th and 20th Centuries seems to have been age of North Atlantic countries. They have worked so hard for their plans for a new world. Those two wineskins now seem to be old, too old for the new age and the new world of nearly 300 independent nations.

The world is changing so fast, so much and in so many ways that we cannot repair some of the old structures to meet our needs today. The door of a new age is opening to us. This is the age of the small, the little and the weak replacing the big and the strong. It could be called the age of the ants or the grasshoppers. I saw big houses of ants in Africa and Latin America. Such small insects were building structures twice as tall as any human being, and strong as a rock.

Maybe the people of the Non-Western World are to be

like those ants and our cooperative network as the house of ants. I certainly believe that if we can join together our strengths and resources, with the help of the Holy Spirit, we will see a miraculous outcome. We have learned from the teaching of the mustard seed in the New Testament and the fearful power of the grasshoppers in the Pentateuch.

We are approaching the age in which we will discover the power of the weak and the poor. The years beyond 2000, may we be the age that will belong to the powerless and the weak of today.

The coming new age is the age when the weak will join together to be the strong, and the weak will disgrace the strong. The new age will be the last age of the Holy Spirit in which the nucleus of life will explode.

III. Transformation of Seminary Curriculum to Mission & Evangelism Centered

I was an honor graduate in theology at the Presbyterian Theological Seminary, Seoul, Korea in June 1949. I began to evangelize in order to plant a church, but I failed to reach nonbelievers. Immediately after graduation, I soon realized I was a failure in evangelism because my seminary training had not taught me how to evangelize the unreached. I then decided to study evangelism and mission and dreamed to alter the seminary curriculum to evangelism centered curriculum.

In 1956 I went to the United States to pursue studies in mission and evangelism. In the 1950s, the Korean Government did not allow people studying abroad to take along their families, and so I was alone until 1960, when I finished my training in the States. I went to the WEC Missionary Training Center in Fort Washington, Pennsylvania, and later to Bethany Missionary College in Minneapolis, Minnesota. I continued my studies under J. T. Seamand (mission) and Robert Coleman (evangelism) at Asbury

Theological Seminary in Wilmore, Kentucky, where I received a Th.M. in mission in 1960. I later received two honorary doctor of divinity degrees: from Belhaven College, in Jackson, Mississippi, and from my alma mater, Asbury Theological Seminary. Finally, in 1993, I earned a Ph.D. in international development at William Carey International University in Pasadena, California.

Beginning in 1961, I advocated for mission & evangelism studies courses at seminaries in Korea. I began to teach mission and evangelism at the Presbyterian Seminary, the Methodist Seminary, and the Holiness Seminary in Seoul.

In 1963 I established the International School of Mission in Seoul, which later, in 1973, expanded to become the East-West Center for Missions Research and Development. It was the first missionary training and research institute in the non-Western world.

IV. Non-Western Missions Network and East-West Cooperation

I dreamed of building a partnership with Western missions to develop leadership for the newly emerging Asian missions. I began making contacts at the Asia Pacific Congress on Evangelism, held in Singapore November 5–13, 1968. While there, I visited the Overseas Missionary Fellowship headquarters, located in Singapore, and shared with the chief executives my vision for cooperating to train missionaries of the Korean mission agencies. After a short discussion, however, they coldly refused my proposal.

I continued to contact Western missions operating in Asia, asking for their cooperation with the newly emerging Asian missions. I traveled to the United States and contacted the Christian and Missionary Alliance (C&MA) mission in New York, where I met Louis King, general secretary of the C&MA board, and proposed that they work together with Korean missionaries in Vietnam. Vietnam was a major mission field of C&MA in Asia, and a number of Korean missionaries had recently begun mission work there. After a long discussion, however, they gently declined my proposal of partnership with Korean missions.

I next went to Wilmington, Delaware, to meet the CEO of the World Presbyterian Mission and propose a partnership, but they also refused. I then went to Wheaton, Illinois, to meet the head of The Evangelical Alliance Mission (TEAM), as I had been heavily involved in the mission's attempts to open the Word of Life Press and mission radio station in Korea. I was also responsible for much of their progress in literature and radio ministries in Korea. TEAM, however, as with the previous missions I had contacted, chose not to accept my proposal of partnership. My yearlong effort to build a partnership with Western missions had failed.

I decided to build an Asia-wide network first and then later pursue contacting Western missions. In 1971 I traveled to twelve Asian countries, meeting with Akira Hatori in Japan, Philip Teng and Timothy Dzao in Hong Kong, David Liao in Taiwan, Witchean Wataki Charowen in Thailand, Chandu Ray in Singapore, G. D. James in Malaysia, and Greg Tingson in the Philippines. I also contacted Doan Vau Mieng in Vietnam and met Samuel Kamaleson and Theodore Williams in India, Bashir Jiwan in Pakistan, and Sabuhas Sangma in Bangladesh.

All were major leaders of the Asian missionary movement in the 1960s. They unanimously agreed to help launch a network of Asian missions and to cooperate in fostering mutual relationships between partners. We finally reached a consensus to call the All-Asia Mission Consultation, which would take place in Seoul in August 1973.

In September 1971 I attended the Green Lake Conference of the Interdenominational Foreign Mission Association (IFMA; now CrossGlobal Link) and the Evangelical Foreign Missions Association (EFMA), where I announced the upcoming All-Asia Mission Consultation planned for August 1973 and gave an open invitation to the leaders of Western missions.

Responses came from the following mission professors and executives: Arthur Glasser, Dean of Fuller Theological Seminary's School of World Mission (now School of Intercultural Studies), Pasadena, California; Ralph Winter and Peter Wagner, professors at Fuller's School of World Mission; George Peters, professor at Dallas Theological Seminary, Dallas, Texas; Edwin (Jack) Frizen, Executive Secretary of IFMA; Clyde Taylor, Executive Secretary of EFMA; Waldron Scott, General Secretary of the World Evangelical Fellowship (WEF); and Horace Williamson, Asia Director of Worldwide Evangelization for Christ (WEC), U.S.A.

With this invitation to high-profile Western mission leaders, I achieved my first step to my goal of cooperation between the East and West for Asian missionary leadership development. The All-Asia Mission Consultation was held in Seoul from August 27 to September 1, 1973. The participants were twenty-six leading figures from thirteen Asian countries; four specially invited Western missiologists; three executives of IFMA, EFMA, and WEF; two representatives from WEC and Wycliffe Bible Translators; and twelve observers from Western missionaries who were working in Korea.

The consultation resolved to form a continuation committee to carry out the following three functions:

(1) sending out at least two hundred new Asian missionaries by the end of 1974;
(2) encouraging the formation of national missions associations in every country of Asia; and
(3) working for the establishment of the East-West Center for Missions Research and Development in Seoul.

The Continuation Committee accomplished all of these functions, including sending two hundred new missionaries before the end of 1974 to two unevangelized areas: Kalimantan Island of Indonesia and northeastern Thailand. In addition, national missions associations were formed in Japan, Korea, Hong Kong, India, and Indonesia before the end of 1974.

The East-West Center for Missions Research and

Development was established immediately after the consultation in 1973, and it opened the first Summer Institute of World Mission on the day following the consultation. Sixty-seven students from five Asian countries were enrolled, and four professors who attended the consultation were invited to be instructors for the Center's first Summer Institute.

As the executive director of the Continuation Committee, I initiated the formation of the Asia Missions Association (AMA), which became the first regional missions association in the world. AMA's inaugural meeting met from August 28 to September 1, 1975, at the Academy House in Seoul, with delegates from thirteen Asian countries: Bangladesh, the Republic of China, Hong Kong, India, Indonesia, Japan, Korea, Malaysia, Pakistan, the Philippines, Singapore, Thailand, and Vietnam; and with Western fraternal delegates from Germany, the Netherlands, the United Kingdom, and the United States.

The inaugural convention of AMA affirmed the Seoul Declaration on Christian Mission, which I drafted and which became a counterpart of the Wheaton Declaration of 1966 and the Frankfurt Declaration of 1970.

AMA grew quickly and was influential even beyond Asia in Africa and Latin America. The Nigeria Evangelical Missions Association was formed by Panya Baba, who attended the second triennial convention of AMA in Singapore in 1978. The Association of Brazilian Cross-Cultural Missions Agencies was formed by Jonathan Santos, who also attended the third triennial convention of AMA in Seoul in 1982.

In addition, the Third World Missions Association was launched in May 1989 as an intercontinental network of missions in Asia, Africa, and Latin America.

Many Western mission leaders took notice of these ventures. I was invited by Billy Graham to join the Preparatory Consultation for the International Congress on World Evangelization, Lausanne, Switzerland, and I was honored to serve as chairperson at the third meeting of the

Preparatory Consultation.

In 1974, I was appointed as a speaker for the plenary session on mission strategy at the congress. In my paper at Lausanne, entitled "Innovation of Mission Structure for the New World," I stressed the need to move away from the one-way mission of the Western world to a two-way approach to missions. I also emphasized that both East and West have needs and resources, and input and output must therefore come from both sides.

The East and the West should join hands in order to research and analyze the availability of resources and the areas of need, and in this way to produce new forces for mission from both worlds.

In these ongoing efforts, the Lord gave me a number of loyal partners from the West to fulfill my dream of East-West cooperation in missionary leadership development.

The first was Donald A. McGavran of Fuller School of World Mission. He encouraged me in an article he wrote in 1972 in the *Church Growth Bulletin*. Even though I did not had the opportunity to meet him personally, he had heard about my efforts to stimulate the missionary movement in Asia and spoke highly of my labors. He came to Seoul in 1974 to teach at the Summer Institute of World Mission, which I had started in 1973. He advised me in my work toward developing Asian leadership in mission. Until his death, he was a loyal supporter of my efforts to bring East and West together in mission cooperation.

The second was Ralph D. Winter, one of my mentor and a partner for the East-West cooperation of mission leadership development. For thirty-six years, from 1973 until his death in May 2009, he was associated with my activities of missionary leadership development and networking of Third World missions. I often requested him to join me in mission work--in Seoul Manila, Thailand, Moscow, Ephesus, and elsewhere--and he never said no. He also never hesitated to write to North Korean leaders, inviting them to William Carey

International University for my peace mission movement with North Korea.

The third special partner in mission has been Dale W. Kietzman. He was the U.S. Director for Wycliffe Bible Translators and became Vice-President of the East-West Center for Missions Research and Development in Seoul, assisting my efforts of East-West cooperation. He served with me since 1974. While he was serving as Executive Vice-President of William Carey International University, he visited North Korea with me three times as my fellow worker for the mission to North Korea. Ralph D. Winter, Dale W. Kietzman, and I were born in 1924 and have ministered together for the advancement of mission from Non-Western world.

From 2000 to 2003 I served as a missionary in Russia. I established the Russian Institute of Christian Leadership Development in Moscow and formed the Moscow Synod of the Church of Christ, Russia, in 2002.

I hosted the eighth triennial convention of the Asia Missions Association, which was held in Moscow in September 2003. I also formed the Asian Society of Missiology, which in 2007 elected Timothy K. Park as its first President. In November 2006 the Ninth Triennial Convention of the Asia Missions Association was held in Ephesus, Turkey. The theme of the convention was "Mission, the Apostolic Way."

The Third World Missions Association (TWMA) initiated to call the Centennial Celebration and Consultation of Edinburgh 1910 in Tokyo. TWMA became a major sponsoring body of Tokyo 2010 Global Consultation and Celebration on May 11 to 15. The coming Tenth Triennial Convention of AMA will be held in Jakarta, Indonesia in November 3 to 7, 2010, hosted by Dr. Jacob Nahuway who was a graduate of the East-West Center for MRD.

AFRICAN MISSIONARY MOVEMENT

Celebration and Evaluation Process of the African Mission Movement – Focus on Ghana

Dr. Seth Anyomi
African Christian Mission

AFRICAN MISSIONARY MOVEMENT

Celebration and Evaluation Process of the African Mission Movement - Focus on Ghana

Africa was once referred to as the "Dark Continent", simply because very little was known about this continent by the Western World. Then, with European exploration in the 15th century and accompanying introduction of the Christian faith, the journey of Africa's discovery began. Six centuries later, Christianity spread rapidly throughout Africa, south of the Sahara and exceeded the west in population in adherents of the Christian faith. Now, the Western Church has a different label for the African Church. It is now referred to as Christianity that is "a mile wide and an inch deep", meaning that Africa has large numbers of believers, but remains shallow in biblical knowledge and the Christian disciplines.

My paper looks at this historical and theological assessment of African Christianity. We will take a look at the Church and Mission models that have evolved along the way. What are their strengths, weaknesses? How well is the African Church fulfilling God's disciple making mandate? And then, is the African Church as a whole ready for the coming of the Lord?

ARRIVAL OF WESTERN MISSIONS

Portuguese explorers and merchants landed on the

West African coast during the second half of the 15Th Century. They came with Catholic Priests on board their ships. The initial contact with the coastal people of West Africa did not yield much in terms of conversions to the Christian faith. In 1880 two men, Eugene Morat and Augustus Morean of the Society of African Mission (SAM) arrived at Elimina in the Gold Coast. Their work was limited to the area around the Portuguese transit Castle. Their work did not have a lasting impact.

In the 1730s two Monrovian Missionaries, Chrettein Protten and Henrich Huckuff arrived in the Gold Coast. Not much can be said in regard to their missionary undertakings.

In 1954 the Church of England Society for the Propagation of the Gospel sent a Missionary, Rev. Thompson to the Cape Coast. It was he who made a first significant attempt to reach the natives. As part of his strategy to win Africans for Christ, he sponsored three native boys to study in the UK. Two of the boys died in the UK and the only survivor, Philip Quacoe was ordained as an Anglican Priest and returned to the Gold Coast to live and do the work of Missions around the Cape Coast area. He was unable to make many converts before his death in 1766. However, he established a school and thus ignited a torch for education that continues to burn bright in the Cape Coast areas, pointing to Cape Coast and surrounding towns as educational centers in Ghana.

Another major Mission group to arrive in Ghana was Basel Missionaries. From 1828 onwards, the Basel Evangelical Missionary Society sent out a team of four Missionaries to the Chritianborg area of Accra. In 1832, three others arrived in the Gold Coast.

Methodism followed with the arrival of Joseph Dunwell in 1835. He died the same year. Two natives, Joseph Smith and William de Graft continued the work until two Missionary couples were sent by the Wesleyan Missionary Society. These couples also died shortly upon their arrival. Next to come was Thomas Birch Freeman, a Mulatto who pushed Wesleyan Missionary work from Cape Coast and its surroundings far inland, reaching into the territory of the Ashantis . In the year 1835, the first Methodist Chapel was built in Cape Coast. A hundred more converts were added within the first two years.

The Church could have spread further north. Political conflicts between the British and the Ashantis caused a suspension of activities in 1872. Active missionary activity resumed by 1900. Kumasi became an established center for the Methodist Church.

From 1847 onwards, Bremen Missionaries arrived and settled on the eastern part of the Gold Coast, later called German Togo. They worked among the Ewe tribe, who were the native settlers in that part of the Gold Coast. Out of the Bremen Mission emerged the present day Evangelical Presbyterian Church.

These Western Missions have impacted the lives and destinies of the people they came to meet on the African coast, most importantly in the areas of Education, Agriculture, Trade, Architecture, Transportation and Health Care.

Due to the excellent educational foundation laid by the early Missionaries, we find Africans excelling in many areas of Religious, academic, political, national and international arenas of life. Africans like Kofi Annan, former Secretary General of the UN, Dr.Setri Nyomi, General Secretary of World Reformed Churches and many others are testimonies of excellence to credit missions in Africa.

It is through the work of early Missions that Tetteh Quarshie of Ghana visited the Island of Fernardo Po, from whence he introduced the cocoa cash crop to Ghana. From then on, Ghana became a great cocoa growing nation and was at one time the leading cocoa producer in the World.

A Basel Missionary called Andrea Riis, first blended

western architecture with local building styles in Ghana. Even today, his influence is seen in the building styles of many Ghanaian homes both in the cities and country side.

The Missionaries introduced road construction and the use of bicycles to enable them to carry the gospel into the hinterland. This writer comes from Amedzofe, one of the places where the early Bremen Missionaries settled. The road they constructed, using human labor to reach the mountain top where they eventually settled, is still in use.

Many of the early missionaries perished from the deadly mosquito bite. This necessitated the introduction of health care both for their well being and that of the people they came to serve.

THE MISSIONARY CHURCHES

Every major Mission agency that worked in different parts of Africa planted a denominational church named after the Church from which their sending Mission was sent. So today, we have Catholic Churches, Anglican Churches, Presbyterian Churches from Basel in Switzerland, the Evangelical Presbyterian Church from northern Germany and the Methodist Churches planted by the Wesleyan Missionaries from England.

THE EMERGENCE OF INDIGENOUS MISSIONS IN GHANA

Africans have worked side by side with the early Western Missionaries sent to bring the gospel to West Africa, such as Phillip Quacoe of Ghana. Prophet Harris, whose work extended through Liberia, Ivory Coast and Ghana. The foundation for future indigenous Missions has been laid, but the Missionary activities we see today began with an Indigenous missionary society called Christian Outreach Fellowship (COF) in the seventies. Encouraged by the work of the Scripture Union Fellowship, the late Honorable

William Ofori Atta founded COF. Later, the Africa Christian Mission, founded by Dr. Seth Kofi Anyomi, was born in the early 1980s. Following these two, many independent and Church sponsored mission initiatives began to emerge. In the beginning, there was a big confusion in differentiating between evangelism and missions. This misunderstanding brought a delay in the understanding and embracing of the emerging mission initiatives of African origin.

THE GHANA EVANGELICAL MISSIONS ASSOCIATION (GEMA)

The founding of GEMA coincided with the first Ghana consultation on Evangelism and Missions, organized by the Ghana Evangelism Committee (GEC). One year earlier, through the encouragement of the Third World Missions Association (TWMA), a Ghanaian Missionary returned home looking for an opportunity to unite the Missionary family. After the presentation on the status of the unfinished task of Missions, Rev. Reuben Ezemadu of the Nigerian Evangelical Missionary Association (NEMA) and the TWMA, told the story of NEMA, to challenge the Ghanaian missionaries and mission Churches to come together. The invitation was well received. The late President to the Methodist convention, Professor Kwasi Dickson was invited to say a prayer for the infant body and GEMA became a national missionary association with Dr. Seth Anyomi as first President.

GEMA, has done a lot to promote Mission awareness in Ghana among the denominational Churches, as well as promote co-operation among missions and mission related bodies. In recent years, GEMA has focused on teaching member organizations how to fund their missions though micro financing.

At the International front, GEMA is well represented both on the TWMA and the WEA. GEMA played a major role on both the Attrition and Retention research projects of the WEA. GEMA's first President chaired the committee that gave birth to the World Link University, became the founding

President and still serves as International Chancellor.

INITIAL PROBLEMS/CHALLENGES FACING INDIGENOUS MISSIONS

The young Mission Agencies were confronted with many difficulties and challenges such as the colonial cliché, in which Christianity is linked with colonialism and seen as a "white man's religion." The native missionaries were also faced with problems of syncretism and that of contextualization.

Indigenous Church/Mission structures and government (authoritarian and bureaucratic) were passed down by Western Missions. They also left behind the capital intensive model of missions.

They seem to pass of the suspicion that has existed between the Western Church and the Mission Agencies that emerged from them.

The attrition study conducted by the WEA, showed clearly that, lack of proper missionary training was a leading factor in Missionary drop out. Lack of proper training also led to faulty theology, methodologies and mismanagement of mission and relative resources.

The African missionary received his education under a European/Western model. What is learned sometimes fails to transfer properly into the African context.

CONTRIBUTION OF AFRICAN MISSIONS TO THE WORLD MISSIONS

First and foremost is the unquestionable numerical strength of the African Church as a whole, over 250 million followers of Christ. Africans are naturally sensitivity to the spirit world in general and the Holy Spirit in particular. It is common knowledge that the African missionary has the ability to endure more pain and hardship than their western counterparts. At the same time Africans live on a fraction of the funds needed to support a western missionary. African migration to western urban centers has led to the establishment of African Churches in Europe and North America. In fact, some of he largest Churches in the western hemisphere are led by African Pastors. The group dynamics of African people, facilitates discipleship making/ mentoring more than the individualistic, self sufficiency model of the western world.

LOOKING INTO THE FUTURE

The Church needs a good definition and understanding of Missions. Church leaders need to be clear that Mission goes beyond evangelism and Church planting. That it encompasses the Great Commission to go "and make disciples of all Nations."

LATIN AMERICAN
MISSIONARY MOVEMENT

Decio de Carvalho
COMIBAM International

LATIN AMERICAN
MISSIONARY MOVEMENT

For the context of this event I will be covering the Latin American missionary movement in some aspects, since that was the theme I was asked to present. But I will also touch on information covering a wider region known as Iberoamerica. COMIBAM has now been working as an Iberoamerican movement for 25 years. It covers 24 Spanish and Portuguese speaking countries in the American continent, the Caribbean and Europe, as well as the Hispanics in the United States and Canada.

I. An Example to Follow – History of the Church in Latin America

As we look at the Latin American Missionary Movement we need to first consider the church in Latin America itself. It is a history of dedication, vision and sacrifice. The first to come where killed before getting off the ships. Those who followed also laid down their lives in obedience to God. Please allow me to abound on this as much as on the other three areas of this presentation. The Iberoamerican Mission Movement, as well as the missionary work being done today across the world by Iberoamerican missionaries, was a result of the vision and commitment of those early missionaries, those who followed them and the pastors and church leaders of the more recent history.

During the first 300 years of the Colonial period, German, French, Dutch and Scottish Protestants established colonies, some with very good results among the general population, while others were more exclusive. But the dominating Roman Catholic Church would not allow it, so the Colonial powers would stop those efforts for a time.

In the early XIX Century, the British Bible Society would send missionaries to begin distributing Bibles throughout Latin America. James (known in Latin America as Diego) Thomson arrived in Argentina in 1819, but would soon move on to Chile, Peru, Ecuador, Mexico and the Caribbean.

Many other British Bible Society missionaries followed Thomson, preaching and distributing a short and economical version of the Reina-Valera Spanish Bible throughout Latin America. At the time, most countries were still dominated by the Roman Catholic Church and there was no freedom of religion.

Many foreign mission entities considered Latin America evangelized, but later realized there was a huge need and opportunity for the Gospel. Around the middle of the XIX Century most countries allowed the establishment of Protestant movements. But it was still a persecuted and lower class minority. However, the missionaries had done and continued to do significant work not only in evangelizing but also in education and medicine, establishing many schools and hospitals. The church was well accepted by the politicians and the governments.

The Evangelical Church in Latin America was young and still very small at the turn of the XIX Century. It is estimated there were about 250.000 Protestants in the whole region in 1900. But there would be phenomenal fruit in the years to come, and nationals would lead those efforts, with the help of many missionaries who continued to come and collaborate in reaching out to the far corners of the continent. The current size of the church in Latin America is estimated at 55 million (1,000,000 % in 100 years).

The following table summarizes these historical events, giving us a clear perspective of the high price paid to bring the Gospel to the nations and peoples of Latin America.

Year	Country	Event
1528	Venezuela	Welser family establishes a Lutheran colony. It became influential and well accepted. Lars Qualben wrote that the whole colony embraced the Lutheran faith. By 1546 it had been dissolved.
1555	Brazil	French Huguenot escapees form a colony near the Guanabara Bay. Disbanded by 1560 by order of the King of Portugal.
1624	Brazil	Dutch Calvinists establish work in Pernambuco. It lasted 30 years, until the Portuguese regained control of the region.
1698	Panama	Scottish Presbyterian colony is established, but fails economically and causes major problem for Scotland. Only lasted 2 years.
1700 - 1800	Several	A number of individuals manage to establish small communities, but are discovered and accused by the inquisition. No evangelical work remains.
1700	Caribbean	Moravians work among the African slaves.
1819	Argentina	After the independence of the colonies, a new era begins. British Bible Society missionary James (Diego) Thomson is well received.
1821	Chile	James (Diego) Thomson arrived in Chile, invited by President Bernardo O'Higgins.

1822	Peru	James (Diego) Thomson arrived in Peru and was appointed national Secretary of Education.
1824	Ecuador	James (Diego) Thomson arrived in Ecuador. He later worked in Mexico and the English and Spanish islands of the Caribbean.
1836	Brazil	Methodist missionaries arrivd, followed by Congregationals in 1855, Presbyterians in 1859 and Baptists in 1881.
1868	Chile	Foundation of the Presbyterian Church .
1892	Mexico	Under persecution, but 566 churches had been established. By 1908 there were 700.
1909	Chile	First indigenous church was established.

II. Not Only a Mission Field, but also a Mission Force – Latin American Missionary Work History

During the Colonial period, when some efforts were made to establish Evangelical churches in Latin America, some nationals were trained to become ministers and evangelists. The early missionaries knew they should make disciples and teach them, so that they too would go out to make more disciples.

When the British Bible Society missionaries came, they quickly decided to look for locals they could train and send out to do Bible distribution itinerant work. They found willing servants, ready to travel long distances on the back of a horse to bring the precious Word of God to very distant and remote areas.

Unfortunately we still do not have a comprehensive work on the history of the Iberoamerican missionary work. We are working on it, so I must say this is a very limited and brief research and most certainly justice will not be made to many across the region who gained a vision for the unreached peoples of the world and went out to bring the Gospel to them.

Based on the information we have gathered so far, early in the 1900's the first denominational national mission entities were established and sent out missionaries. The Brazilian Baptist Convention sent out a Portuguese born believer as a missionary to his own country. This was followed in 1925 by a Brazilian sent as a missionary to Portugal. The Brazilian Presbyterian Church sent their first missionary, also to Portugal, in 1910. In 1916, the Latin American Cooperation Council organized a conference in Panama to discuss mission work in Latin America. This was a reaction to Edinburgh 1910 because at that well known event they did not include missionaries serving in Latin America or leaders of the church in the region due to pressure from certain sectors. They accepted the concept that Latin America was already evangelized by the Catholics, and Protestant missionaries going there were fanaticals and illiterate. The Panama congress contributed to the expansion of the missionary vision of the church in Latin America.

Non-denominational mission societies followed soon after. In 1928 an indigenous mission was founded in Brazil, Missão Caiuá, with the specific aim of reaching the tribal groups of the country. In 1946, in Peru, Juan Cuevas founded AMEN, an indigenous non denominational mission organization, focused on reaching the unreached towns and peoples of Peru. This agency would soon begin to look beyond and work to see Peruvian and other Latino missionaries serving in Europe. In the years that followed, other denominational mission efforts were initiated in countries such as Argentina, Chile, Venezuela, Puerto Rico and Cuba.

But only a few non denominational organizations existed until the mid 70's. In Brazil, Jonathan dos Santos and Decio Azevedo, challenged by missionary and mission teacher Barbara Burns, established Missão Antioquia in 1976, with a focus on mobilization, training and sending of missionaries to unreached countries. In 1982 an indigenous, Latino formed, interdenominational and international organization would be established in Spain, focusing on work in North Africa.

More mission entities were being established, more churches were participating and more missionaries were going to more places. There was a need to communicate and cooperate, and the first steps were taken to form national mission networks. The Brazilian Mission Association is established officially in 1982. Mexico forms a similar entity in 1987 and Argentina follows in the early 90's.

In 1984, Luis Bush and a few other pastors in Central America begin to consider the idea of a major continental and international mission congress. The plan takes shape and in 1987 the First Iberoamerican Mission Congress takes place in São Paulo, Brazil. More than 3,000 attended the event, representing almost every country in the continent. Other mission mobilization events had happened in several countries, but none had been as focused and challenging. At the end of the congress, Luis Bush and those in the organizing committee drafted a declaration. The main statement of the document was simply "Iberoamerica is not only a mission field now, but also a mission force".

In 1997 the Second Iberoamerican Mission Congress took place in Mexico, and in 2006 the third congress was organized in Spain. These events were known as COMIBAM, and by 2000 a decision was made to establish an international Iberoamerican collaboration entity under the name of COMIBAM Internacional. Many other national, regional and thematic events have been organized over the years.

This brief history could be presented in short by viewing it in the following five periods:

1. Early post colonial period: 1840 – 1900 In country, focused on Jerusalem and Samaria – entirely done by denominations

2. Initial international mission efforts: 1900 – 1950

International, but mostly within the neighboring countries or culturally related – founding of the first non-denominational agencies

3. First response to the challenge and opportunities: 1950 – 1980 Significant mobilization, recruiting, training and sending to the most needy and unreached people groups - forming of national networks

4. Growth and expansion: 1980 – 2000 Entering some of the so called "creative access" countries, but better equipped due to the establishing of mission focused training programs, fast increase of sending structures and missionaries - forming of an international Iberoamerican cooperation

5. Partnership unto the ends of the earth: 2000 and onwards – Maturing, focus on the field and the missionary - Forming of alliances with other international networks.

Recognizing once again the limited research done so far in this area, the following table summarizes these historical events and lets us take a first look at the first steps taken by the Iberoamerican church in the process of becoming a missionary movement.

Year	Country	Event
1908	Brazil	Brazil Brazilian Baptist Convention supported North American and indigenous missionary in Chile. In 1911 the Brazilian Baptist Mission Board sent their first missionary to Portugal, followed by a second worker in 1925.
1910	Brazil	The Brazilian Presbyterian church sent a missionary to Portugal.
1916	Panama	Latin American Cooperation Council conference was held. (reaction to Edinburgh 1910)

1928	Brazil	Missão Evangélica Caiuá – An indigenous agency focused on reaching the tribal peoples of Brazil. Another agency with a similar vision, MEVA, was established in 1948.
1946	Peru	Juan Cuevas - AMEN
1976	Brazil	Jonathan dos Santos & Decio Azevedo – Missão Antioquia.
1976	Brazil	Eude Martins established CEBIMI – Centro Brasileiro de Informação Missionária. The first meeting to create AMTB, which was officially established in 1982.
1982	Spain	Pablo Carrillo - PMI
1987	Mexico	COMIMEX
1987	Brazil	COMIBAM I – About 300 known missionaries
1997	Mexico	COMIBAM II – Around 4000 missionaries
2000	Peru	I COMIBAM International Assembly
2006	Spain	COMIBAM III – 9265 missionaries

III.   Under Construction – Current State of Latin American Missionary Work

The information presented at a meeting in Bombay in 1977 to international mission leaders indicated there were 136 Latin Americans serving as overseas missionaries.

There has been significant growth, but we all agree that we would love to see so much more happening. Since 1995 COMIBAM has carried out periodic statistical research to gather information on the state of the movement. From 286 mission entities in 1996, in 2006 we found that the number had grown to 462.

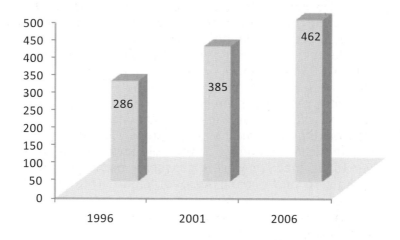

In 1996 there were about 3900 missionaries, having grown from an estimated 300 in 1987. In 2006 there were 9265. Ted Limpic, who coordinated these research projects, estimates that at the current pace, and even considering an expected slowing down, there may be as many as 32,000 Iberoamerican missionaries serving cross-culturally by 2020.

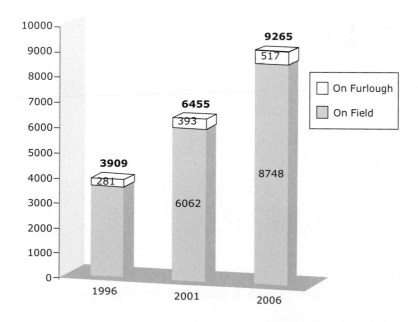

The research is thorough and offers so much information, including countries of origin, countries of service, types of sending organizations, and more. It is available at the COMIBAM site at http://www.comibam.org/catalogo2006/index_i.htm.

More recently, in preparation for the third congress, a second major research project was launched, this time seeking to examine more closely the state of the Iberoamerican missionary at the field level. It had become clear to us that we were discussing, planning, praying, strategizing and organizing events, but forgetting that those who actually do the work are the missionaries. An online survey was prepared and carried out among 1,100 Iberoamerican missionaries, covering a well predefined range of age, gender, marital status, denominational background, length of stay and other important characteristics. This document was published in 2006 under the name Strengths and Weaknesses of the Iberoamerican Missionary. It can be found at the COMIBAM site at http://comibam.org/docs/report_research_en.pdf.

We consider the movement one that is still young, and therefore prone to mistakes. It is a work under construction, God being the builder.

IV. Collaboration – The Future of Latin American Missionary Work

I wanted to conclude this with a brief look at the future. Where are we going and how do we get there? I must point out that COMIBAM is not an association. It is also not a representative of the Iberoamerican or Latinamerican entire mission endeavor. The organization exists to serve and to offer a venue for dialogue and collaboration among those national missions bodies and other mission entities in the region.

Leadership
God has raised a great number of capable and

committed people in Iberoamerica for missionary work; pastors and church leaders, professionals, business people and mission candidates. We are excited about the future. There is still significant work to be done in the area of mobilization, and that is currently our largest focus area.

Intercession

This has been a strong emphasis in our movement during the past 10 years. We were late, but the Koreans had a huge influence on us and there are now mission prayer initiatives throughout Iberoamerica. But we still need to expand in this area, we need to be more dynamic in passing on information, in calling prayer gatherings and in teaching the ordinary Christians in our part of the world to be effective intercessors.

Focus

During these past two decades, and even looking back to the first years of the Iberoamerican movement, there has been a strong emphasis on the unreached or the least reached. This has helped give focus and maintain a high level of interest. Concepts and programs such as the 10/40 Windows, the Adopt a People and the major religious blocks of the world are taken into account by the mission entities throughout the region when considering their current and future strategies.

Children and youth

In Iberoamerica we are facing the same issues as in other parts of the world. Our people have travelled and seen how the young generations, and even the children, from across the planet, are quickly being impacted by the modern societies they live in. They are all familiar with the computer and the mobile phone, the internet, TV and so much more. Their language now includes googling, facebooking and texting. We have noticed it is harder to get them to consider a missionary trip and a commitment to missions these days. At the same time, the average age of population in our countries continue to drop, and so is the age of the average mission candidate. Our response has been to look at the children and youth in Iberoamerica and dedicate time and effort to relate to them and communicate the Great Commission in a way they understand. And we are letting young leaders do this. We also want young leaders involved in the overall mission work in Iberoamerica.

Women

Another huge area is that of women. In our case, the numbers show that they are a majority in the mission field and very significant work has been done over the year by single women and by the wives. However, there is very little focus on their needs and capabilities, and there is little room for them to participate in leadership. We have recognized our failure in this area and have launch discussions to make changes and to implement a women initiative within the movement

Training

Adequate training has been a strong need and an area of very intensive work in Iberoamerica. We are in the process of researching our training schools and their content, but our most recent numbers indicated close to 200 mission training centres. After years of work we have now published the *Best Practices Guide for Missionary Training in Iberoamerica*. The world is changing rapidly, socially, economically, demographically and in many other ways. The missionaries of tomorrow will not be ready to be effective in the mission field if we continue to train them like we did yesterday. Our next strong effort in the area of equipping is to see an expansion in the practical and professional training programs, which need to come alongside the theological and missiological training being offered.

Practical Help for Sending Structures

The number of mission agencies and sending structures will continue to grow. Another aspect of this is that more and more local churches are sending missionaries and getting involved directly in mission fields across the world. These organizations and churches need very practical help to be able to adequately function as a sending structure, able to provide the needed support and services for the missionary and the ministry in the field. This is another area of focus and we have plans to organize some events to generate dialogue and to eventually create a set of practical tools for the sending structures.

Practical Help for the Iberoamerican Missionary

As the number of missionaries serving across the world grows, and the world continues to change dramatically, so will the very practical situations the workers face and their needs. This is an area we have been weak at. With our big push to mobilize more churches, see more sending structures and more missionaries being sent, we did not consider the specific aspects of life in the mission field. Along with the already mentioned field oriented research project carried out before the 2006 congress in Spain, missionaries themselves were brought to the event (300 of them) so that we would have their input in every aspect of the thinking and strategising that would take place there. After the publication of the research report, our 8 regions have been looking at the results and several national mission movements have also carried out gatherings to consider these and to help the mission entities in their countries apply the conclusions to their current missions practice. Looking forward, internationally we will be introducing a program to help Iberoamerican families with the educational needs of their children and another to promote advanced and continuous education programs for the missionary.

More Research

In COMIBAM we are committed to doing it well, and we know that takes work and requires good information. There are several more research projects already planned or in the planning stages. These will again be invaluable for the whole movement and for those we work along with.

We were born out of a vision of cooperation and collaboration to accomplish the missionary task. This is what led to the expansion of the Iberoamerican missionary work in the 80's and 90's. But God has raised and is using His church from areas of the world we have not had much contact with over the years, such as Africa, Asia and Eastern Europe. We are committed to forming new relationships and establishing alliances that will enable all of us to advance quickly. We are in dialogue with national and international networks such as CrossGlobal Link, in the US and the European Evangelical Mission Association, and already have a collaboration agreement with MANI – Movement of African National Initiatives. We are convinced that together we can do it not only faster, but also better, and in a John 17 way – the God honouring way.

Bibliography

1. Qualben, Lars P.; *A History of the Christian Church*, décima edición, publicada por Thomas Nelson & Sons, Nueva York, Estados Unidos de América, 1942.

2. Vila, Samuel y Santamaría, Darío; *Enciclopedia Ilustrada de Historia de la Iglesia*, Libros CLIE, Barcelona, España, 1989. ISBN 84-7228-447-6

3. Bianchi, Daniel; Latin America in Mission, 2010

4. PM Internacional; Latinos en Misión, 2008

5. Bertil Ekström; Historia da AMTB

6. COMIBAM Internacional; Strengths and Weaknesses of the Iberoamerican Missionary, 2006

7. COMIBAM Internacional; Missionary Organizations of Ibero-America, 2006

8. Escobar, Samuel; Edimburgo 1910 y los evangélicos iberoamerican

ASIAN MISSIONARY MOVEMENT

Missionary Movement
of Asian Churches

Dr. Timothy K. Park
Fuller Theological Seminary
East-West Center for MRD

East-West
Mission Forum

ASIAN MISSIONARY
MOVEMENT

Missionary Movement
of Asian Churches

In the past, the missionary work was considered solely the western church's business. The churches of the world, however, have realized that Christ's mandate—"Make disciples of all nations"—is for the whole Church on earth. The Asian churches, like churches in other continents, have been involved in missionary works, although their stories have not yet been heard. For instance, the Korean church with a hundred plus years of mission history has been constantly involved in cross-cultural missionary work since 1907.

The characteristics of missionary works of the Asian churches are unique. In this paper, I will briefly present an overview of the missionary movement of the Asian churches and emphasize the distinctiveness of the Asian mission in general. I will also describe the missionary movement of the Korean Church comprehensively as a case study of the Asian mission.

I. MISSIONARY MOVEMENT OF THE KOREAN CHURCH

The Korean Church has been a missionary church almost from the beginning. Currently, the Korean Church has become the second largest missionary-sending church in the world,[1] and is leading the missionary movement of the Asian churches.

A. Brief History of the Korean Church Mission

The mission history of the Korean church can be divided into three periods: (1) mission during the Japanese colonial rule (1907-1957); (2) mission after the independence of Korea (1955-1991); and (3) the current mission (1980-present). Each period is unique in terms of its characteristics.

Mission During Japanese Colonial Period (1907-1957): The Korean Church's missionary work outside of the Korean peninsula began as early as 1907, when the self-¬supporting, self-governing Presbytery of the Presbyterian Church in Korea was formed. As the first native Presbytery was constituted, seven men, the first graduates of the Theological Seminary of Korea, were ordained as ministers. Yi Ki-Poong, one of the seven, was commissioned to Jeju Island[2] as the first Korean Protestant missionary. A missionary committee was appointed to administer the missionary effort, and the presbytery ordered the whole Church to make a special offering for this work of propagating the Christian faith.[3]

The missionary movement of the Korean Church gradually won the support of the believers, and the Church sent missionaries to other parts of the world. In 1909, the church ordained a second group of nine ministers. The Church sent one of them, Choi Kwan-Heul, as a missionary to Vladivostock, Siberia. In the same year, the Presbytery also sent Han Suk-Jin to minister to the Korean students in Tokyo, and Pang Hwa-Chung to minister to the Korean emigrants in California and Mexico.[4]

In 1912, the Presbyterian Church in Korea made a

---

1. NorimitsuOnishe, "Korean Missionaries Carrying Word to Hard-to-Sway Places," *New York Times*, November 1, 2004.

2. Jeju is an island about sixty miles off the southern coast of the mainland of Korea. It was known to foreigners as the Island of Quelpart.

3. George Lak-Geoon Paik, *The History of Protestant Missions in Korean 1832¬-1910*. Seoul, Korea: Yunsei University Press. 1929.

4. Paik 1929: 390; Northern Presbyterian Report for 1910, p. 281.

resolution to send three ministers to Shantung, China—
the birthplace of Confucius and Mencius—to mark the
organization of the General Assembly. In the following year in
1913, the three ministers went into the mission field. "Again,
as an expression of the joy of the Church in the great event,
a 'thank offering' was taken throughout Korea and the three
pastors and their families were sent to open a real foreign
mission work in the Chinese language for the Chinese in
Shantung, China."[5]

The Korean Church sent about eighty missionaries
outside the Korean peninsula during the Japanese colonial
regime. The missionaries were sent to Jeju Island, Siberia,
Japan, California, Mexico, Manchuria, Shantung, Shanghai,
Nanking, Peking, and Mongolia, among others. Most of
the missionaries were sent to minister to the Korean
immigrants in other countries. Some of them also engaged in
evangelizing the natives and the second-generation Koreans,
whose languages and cultures were vastly different from the
people in Korea.

The most significant of the Korean Church's missions
was its mission to Shantung, China, because it was the first
to be solely focused on the natives. In fact, it was the first
mission carried out by Asian people to other Asian people,
since the days of the apostles. Though Korea was a destitute,
powerless nation, the Korean Church sent a message across
the globe that even a young, poor, and powerless non-
western church could carry on a hefty load of missionary
responsibilities.

Unlike the western churches and today's Korean
churches, the Presbyterian Church in Korea dispatched her
missionaries to Shantung, China in consultation with the
American Presbyterian Mission that began work there already
and with the approval of the Chinese Church. They worked in
the areas where both the Chinese Church and the American
Presbyterian Mission assigned them. They, unlike many of
today's Korean missionaries, did not transplant their home
church in the field. They transferred their membership to
the Chinese Church, and served as members of the Chinese

5. C. A. Clark, "The Missionary Work of the Korean Presbyterian
Church," *Korean Mission Field*, (Ed. Ellasue Wagner) Vol. XXX, No. 8, August
1934.

Church.

They worked in harmony with fellow Korean missionaries and in partnership with the Chinese Church and the foreign missions in the field. After their country's loss of sovereignty to Japan, the Korean missionaries carried on their missionary responsibilities from the position of weakness. Denominations played a major role in the missionary movement of the church during the Japanese colonial rule.

Mission After Independence of Korea (1955-1991): After World War II, the missionary movement of the Korean Church was greatly hindered due to political strife in the Far East. The Communist Revolution in the Mainland China and the Korean War compelled the Church to temporarily suspend its missionary work. Although Korea was restored of its sovereignty in 1945, the country still suffered from the consequences of war. Nevertheless, the Korean Church soon resumed its missionary work.

Thus, the missionaries during the three decades after Korean Independence carried out their responsibilities without any strong political, ecclesiastical, or financial support. They also carried on their missionary responsibilities from a position of weakness. During this period, most worked under or in partnership with the western missions, as well as with the churches within their mission fields.

Current Korean Mission—Mission in Affluence (1980-Present): This period can be characterized as "mission in affluence." Multiple factors contributed to the phenomenon, including explosive church growth, economic growth, increase in immigration, improved diplomacy, higher education, and accumulated missionary experience. These factors, among others, have enhanced the missionary movement of the Korean Church in recent years. Abundant resources of Korea, however, were not always beneficial. A rise in wealth also brought negative consequences, such as an increased dependence on material resources than on the Holy Spirit and the Word. In doing so, receiving natives were inadvertently taught to depend on the missionaries and their material resources.

B. Current Situation of the Korean Mission

The Korean Church has emerged as a new missionary force in the 20th century and has aggressively launched its missionary enterprise into the world. There is a strong sense among church leaders that the Lord is using the Korean Church to usher in his kingdom.

Number of Korean Missionaries: According to a survey recently conducted by the Korea World Missions Association, 20,840 Korean missionaries are working in 169 other countries as of January 30, 2010.[6]

Increase of Korean Missionaries

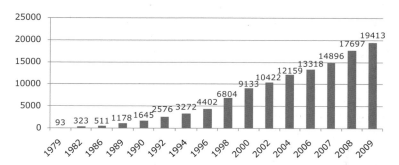

Kinds of Missionaries: In terms of years of service, the number of career missionaries who have served more than three years is 20,819 (94% of total missionaries), and the number of short-term missionaries[7] is 1,311 (6%). While the number of short-term missionaries is increasing gradually, the number of career missionaries increases at a greater rate. In terms of vocation, the number of ordained ministers, including spouses, is 14,697 (66% of total number of missionaries), while the number of lay missionaries is 7,433 (or 34% of the total). The proportion of ordained to non-ordained missionaries is significant.

---

6. They are sent by 96 Korean denominations and 229 Korean missions at home and abroad. *Korea Missions Quarterly*, Vol. 9, N. 3, Spring 2010. P. 79.

7. Short Term Missionaries in this statistics are those who serve in the fields less than three years. Those who visit fields for a couple of weeks are not counted.

Countries in Which the Korean Missionaries Are Working: Geographical data of Korean missionaries shows that 5,760 (26% of total number of missionaries) are working in Northeast Asia (7 countries) including AX and Japan. 3,810 (17.2%) are in Southeast Asia (11 countries), 1,724 (7.8%) are in Central Asia (10 countries), 1,191 (5.4%) are in South Asia (6 countries), 1,030 (4.7%) are in Eastern Europe and Eurasia (22 countries), 1,038 (4.7%) are in Western Europe (18 countries), 2,325 (10.5%) are in North America and Caribbean Countries (6 countries), 842 (3.8%) are in Latin America (19 countries), 897 (4.1%) are in South-East Africa (20 countries), 349 (1.6%) are in Central and West Africa (20 countries), 809 (3.7%) are in North Africa and Middle East (18 countries), 760 (3.4%) are in the Pacific/Oceania (11 countries), 240 (1.1%) are classified as missionaries-at-large and non-residential missionaries, 1,355 (6.1%) are missionaries in home-assignment, apprenticeship, and furlough.[8]

Geographical Data of the Korean Missionaries

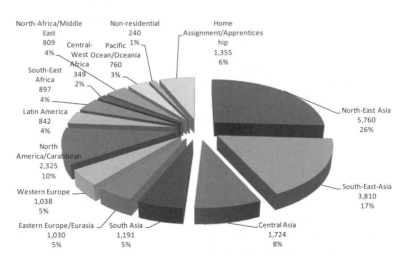

Major Changes of the Korean Mission: Major changes in the Korean missionary movement have occurred in the last three decades.

---

8. *KMQ*, Spring 2010, pp. 80-81.

a. The Korean missionary works in the 1970s were among people group where missionary breakthrough was made and immigrants in other countries. Today, however, the majority of Korean missionaries are involved in cross-cultural missions, particularly among the unreached people groups.

b. Another change is the emergence of native Korean mission organizations. After the independence of Korea, most Korean missionaries worked under the western mission groups. Today, the number of Korean missionaries who work under 96 Korean denominations such as Global Mission Society and 229 native missions such as UBF, Global Partners, GMF, Paul Mission, INTERCP, etc. is much greater than the number of those in the western organizations.

c. During Japan's colonial rule and immediately after the independence of Korea, the missionary movement was carried on mainly through denominations and local churches, with the exception of a few mission organizations. Today, however, the movement has been carried on both by denominational missions and mission organizations. The number of Korean missionaries sent by mission organizations is slightly greater today than that sent by denominations.

d. Another change in Korean mission after 1980s is the in the Korean church's mission from "mission from a position of weakness" to "mission from a position of strength." During Japan's colonial rule and after the Korean War, the missionaries carried out their responsibilities from a position of weakness. During the last three decades, however, they carried out their responsibilities from a position of strength. Instead of relying on the life-changing power of the Holy Spirit and the Word of God, Korean missionaries today tend to rely on the material resources of the Korean Church.

C. Contributing Factors to the Growth of the Korean Mission

Various factors have contributed to the missionary movement of the Korean Church. They include divine, human, organizational and contextual factors.

Divine Factors: Manifestations of the power of God, including revival movements, kept missions growing.

a. Revival movements, particularly the Great Revival Movement in Pyongyang in 1907, contributed to the growth of mission. Because of the fire of spiritual movements, the Korean Church experienced a dynamic vigor in sending missionaries out to surrounding nations. It was customary for the Korean Church to have two revival meetings every year, in the spring and the fall. This tradition helped keep the Korean Church spiritually strong.

b. Manifestations of the power of God and of the Holy Spirit also contributed to the widespread missionary movement. Healings of the sick were often seen in the missionary works on the Island of Jeju.

Human Factors: Human factors, such as a spirit of gratitude and capable leaders are notable contributions to the growth of mission of the Korean Church.

a. Koreans by nature are a people who pay a debt of gratitude when they are shown grace. When the Presbyterian Church in Korea dedicated one out of seven of its first ordained ministers as missionary to the Island of Jeju, they were expressing their joy and gratitude to God for founding the Presbytery in 1907. The sending of three missionary families to Shantung, China was also an expression of gratitude to God for establishment of the General Assembly of the Presbyterian Church of Korea, and to China, where they learned the ethical standards of Confucius and Mencius. On both occasions, the

Church collected a "thank offering" throughout the nation to support these missionaries.

b. There were many capable leaders in the Korean Church who made great impacts on the Korean missionary movement. Rev. Kil Sun-Choo, one of the Presbyterian Church in Korea's first ordained pastors, Dr. Helen Kim of Ewha Woman's University, Dr. David J. Cho of Korea International Mission, Dr. John E. Kim of Chongshin University, Joon Gon Kim of the Korea Campus Crusade for Christ, and Tai-Woong Lee of Global Missionary Fellowship are among those who made significant contributions to the growth of Korean mission.

Organizational Factors: From the outset, the Korean Church created a mission committee to organize and coordinate missionary works. The Church also collaborated with the western mission groups. The Korean student groups also played a significant role in contributing to the movement.

a. Much of the success of today's growth of mission in the Korean Church is due to the organization of missions committees. By creating structures, the missionary works were simultaneously conducted according to the church's structure (modality) and mission's structure (sodality). When one group was in need of support, the other undertook those responsibilities. In recent years, hundreds of native missions have emerged. Some examples are the Korea World Mission Council (KWMC), Korea World Mission Association (KWMA), World Korean Missionary Fellowship (WKMF), and Mission Korea (MK). These groups have facilitated much of the missionary movement in the past three decades.

b. The missions committee of the early Korean Church comprised of both the Korean and the western missionaries. The western missionaries mentored the Korean missionaries and helped them to enter into the new mission fields. Unlike today's missionaries, the early missionaries often worked in partnership with the western mission organizations and the national churches, especially in China.

c. Students have played a crucial role in the widespread growth of the Korean mission. During the Japanese colonial rule, students organized missionary societies and sent or supported missionaries. After Korea's independence from Japan, students at Ewha Woman's university, Chongshin University, and Daejon University among others started their own student missionary movement. Since 1990, Mission Korea (Chul Ho Han) has held bi-annual mission conferences for students and young Koreans. About 45,000 students have attended the conferences held by Mission Korea and among them, 29,000 have made commitments to serve as missionaries in 2008 alone.

Contextual Factors: The contextual factors that have contributed to the spread of the Korean mission movement are: increased Korean immigration, growing influence of the international missionary movements, spread of information, Korea's burgeoning economy, and improved diplomatic ties with foreign nations.

a. Immigration Growth: Political, social and economic conditions in Korea have led to a rise in immigration to countries all over the world. Through immigration, Korean emigrants have become a great missionary force. "Wherever Korean Christians have gone, their churches have accompanied or followed them for the quickening of the peoples among whom they have come to live. This is true to the North in Manchuria and Siberia, to the South on the Island of Jeju, to the West in Shantung, China, and to the East in Hawaii, Mexico, on the west coast of America, and among the Korean students in the city of Tokyo."[9] Korean emigrants and residents have served as missionary forces for the evangelization of the world.

b.   International Conferences: The success of Korea's missionary movement is connected to international conferences. For example, the first mission to China was strengthened by the International Missionary Council held in Edinburgh in 1910 and the mission to Thailand was related to the work of the World Council of Churches.

c.   Information Distribution: The spread of information through newspapers and magazines has stimulated Christians to be aware of their missionary responsibility and has served as a call to action. The Korea Mission Field, a monthly publication by the Evangelical Missions in Korea, was distributed to foreign missionaries in Korea and to their sending and supporting bodies. The Christian Messenger, a weekly joint-publication by Methodists and Presbyterians in Korea, was also used as a great informational source. These newspapers shared news about missionaries and their works with the public. The Christian Messenger stirred up the missionary spirit within the Korean Church by printing an article about the missionary David Livingstone in forty-four consecutive issues. This newspaper also published news about Korean missionaries in other countries. Today, many Christian newspapers and mission journals distribute information about Korean missionary works in many nations.

d.   Burgeoning Economic Growth: With the dynamic growth of the Church, Korea's economy has also achieved an incredible growth during the last decade. Abundant material resources of Korea have had both positive and negative effects on Korean

9. C. A. Clark, "Korean Student Work in Tokyo," Korea Mission Field, Vol. XI. No. 7, July 1915.

mission.

e. Diplomatic Ties with Foreign Nations: Korea's economic growth and successful hosting of the Seoul Olympic Games in 1988 created opportunities for Korea to establish diplomatic ties with almost all nations in the world. Doors were opened wide and today Koreans can travel almost anywhere with a Korean passport.

D. Strengths and Weaknesses of the Korean Mission

Like any organization, the Korean missionary movement has its strengths and weaknesses.

Strengths include: (a) dynamic church growth; (b) ample financial resources; (c) widespread Korean diaspora; (d) strong diplomatic ties with foreign nations; (e) high levels of education; (f) long mission history; and (g) deep passion, courage and commitment for the cause of the Great Commission.

Weaknesses include: (a) an unbalanced mission theology; (b) mono-cultural perspective; (c) lack of field research; (d) inappropriate missionary deployment; (e) improper selection and training of missionaries; (f) competitive individualism; (g) weak administration of mission organizations; and (h) lack of cooperation among the sending, receiving, and supporting bodies.

While remaining faithful to the preaching and teaching of God's Word, the Korean Church has in some aspects neglected its social responsibilities. Many leaders have become church-oriented instead of kingdom-oriented. It is imperative that the leaders preach the gospel in both word and deed. Theology produces methodology. The Korean Church must practice a mission theology that incorporates all spheres of society, including politics, business, media, culture, and education.

The Korean culture is in essence mono-cultural. This creates a tendency for missionaries to impart their culture to the people and the churches they serve. It is important to respect the host cultures and communicate the gospel in a way the natives can accept. Unfortunately, some Korean missions and missionaries work without accurate information or a workable strategy for their fields.

Many missionaries have also been inappropriately selected, trained, and deployed. This results in a lack of cooperation, creating problems of competition among missionaries in the field. Local church pastors who may not have proper knowledge and experience are often in a position of control over their missionaries and their ministries.

Summary

The Korean Church has been a missionary church almost from the beginning of the church. The Korean missionaries are willing to go to any place of the world risking their lives for Christ even to the hardest-to-evangelize corners of the world. The Korean Church's bold faith projection to send one million tent-making missionaries by 2020 and 100,000 career missionaries by 2030 continues to challenge Korean believers around the world. The Korean Church is expected to play an important and unique role in the missionary movement in the 21st century.

Although the Korean Church only received the gospel at the end of the 19th century, it started its cross-cultural mission in the early 20th century—showing churches around world that even a young church can get involved in the missionary work. The Korean Church reconfirmed the biblical principles that even a destitute church suffering under persecution can carry missionary responsibility, and that the work of the lay people is important in the world evangelization. The Church showed that spontaneous ministry of the gospel by lay people, translation of the Bible into native languages, practice of indigenous church planting, thorough teaching of the Bible, right selection and on-the-job training of workers, revival and spiritual renewal, and mission from a position of weakness are essential.

PARTNERSHIP IN MISSIONS RESEARCH AND DEVELOPMENT

Retrospect and Prospect of the Ministries
of US Center for World Mission
& William Carey International University
as Research and Leadership Development

Dave Datema
US Center for World Mission

PARTNERSHIP IN MISSIONS
RESEARCH AND DEVELOPMENT

Retrospect and Prospect of the Ministries
of US Center for World Mission
& William Carey International University
as Research and Leadership Development

INTRODUCTION

I am very honored to stand on Korean soil for the first time. I am especially interested in Korea for two reasons. First, at the US Center for World Mission, all of our members meet once a week in small groups to hold each other accountable to various aspects of the Christian walk. My two colleagues that make up my group are Korean-Americans. Every Thursday morning we drive from Pasadena to Korea Town and eat Salongton. On the way down and back we ask each other questions about our lifestyle, purity issues and witness. During the meal we share about our reading from the Bible or ways that God is teaching us. One of my colleagues has told me that when he was young he went to a restaurant here in Korea and there was a cow head sitting at the entrance, signifying tomorrow's food. So I am looking for a restaurant with a cow head!

The other reason for my interest in Korea comes from my wife. My wife was born and raised in the farm country of rural Ohio, and is culturally a great distance from Korean culture. Yet for some reason, she has a great interest in Korean language and culture. It started when she began watching Korean dramas and she has become interested in the Korean culture that is portrayed in those dramas. Sometimes late at night I will find her sitting at the computer whispering softly Korean words as she tries to read Korean script.   She is presently reading a book called "Awakening the Hermit Kingdom: Pioneer American Women Missionaries in Korea" by Katherine H. Lee Ahn, Adjunct Professor at Fuller Theological Seminary in Pasadena.   Part of the book describes some of the first missionary doctors to Korea. By coincidence, at the same time she started watching a drama called "Jejungwon".   Jejungwon is the name of the Government Hospital which opened in 1885 with the full support and approval of the Korean royal court.   It was the first modern/western hospital in Korea.   The American physician who helped to found the hospital is Dr. Horace Allen, a medical missionary, who gained favor from the royal court when he saved the life of the queen's nephew.   My wife tells me that the book almost reads like a script to the drama.   So I joke with people and I tell them that I have a Korean wife. Also, my next door neighbors are a Korean-American family whose children are close friends with my own children.   All this to say that Korea is not just another country to me, but is a unique place of interest.

It is a great honor to stand at this lectern among the great scholars who have already stood here. They have earned the right to speak due to their academic labors.   I, on the other hand, am here on the basis of my new role as successor to Dr. Ralph Winter as the General Director of the Frontier Mission Fellowship, the legal entity that oversees William Carey International University, the US Center for World Mission, the Roberta Winter Institute and Judson International School.   This new role has taken me places where I don't belong and placed me alongside scholars with whom I can't compete. However, since this paper has to do with my own organization, I feel qualified enough to share some thoughts with you.   This paper is a case study of William Carey International University and the US Center for World Mission. We are but one piece of God's great mosaic of organizations devoted to mission.   As such, we have a great interest in research and leadership development, so I trust that my words will find application to your own organizations that you represent and that there would be many lines of convergence.

RETROSPECT

As I think back on the 35-year history of both the US Center for World Mission and William Carey International University, I am struck by the undying presence of two things: ideas and influence. Of course, our organizations have at their core one central figure, Ralph D. Winter. He was a scholar fond of ideas, but he was also an activist with a deep desire to influence. He downplayed his identity as a scholar and will perhaps be remembered more as a mission activist. Yet this solitary man recruited a small band of dedicated workers who helped turn ideas into new initiatives, whose influence went far beyond where he alone could have taken them. He would never have done it without them. In the Retrospect section of this paper, I want to draw out some principles that I believe best explain our history. As a mission agency dedicated especially to the frontiers of mission, I trust this exercise will serve as a helpful case study of one organization, and that it may prove helpful to you, many of whom represent similar agencies.

1. Ideas must be accompanied by innovation

Without innovation, the group of organizations I represent would never have been started. While Dr. Winter made a name for himself somewhat because of his ideas, most of what he is known for today is more accurately called innovation.

Like anyone with a strong academic background, Winter was fond of ideas and championed many of them, a good number of which were not original to him. He is perhaps most remembered for three core ideas. First would be Theological Education by Extension (TEE), getting education to those already IN ministry, not just young men who might be good pastors someday. This idea came directly from his field experiences as a missionary in Guatemala. The second idea was also original to him, that being the modality/sodality distinction, referring to church and mission structures and the significance of each in their distinct role in advancing God's Kingdom. This idea was first presented in a paper delivered here in Seoul in 1973. This single idea has had a powerful influence in the mission world. In the 1990's Winter testified in a Canadian court case that resulted in the understanding that Protestant mission agencies are in fact Protestant religious orders. The Canadian court ended up agreeing with Winter's position and Revenue Canada ended up with a position very similar to the U.S. IRS, both recognizing special designation for such mission agencies as Protestant religious orders. Third, he is perhaps most remembered for his address in Lausanne in 1974, where he stressed the need for a new ki nd of evangelism to cross cultural barriers to reach peoples. While Donald MacGavran was pointing out those who could be reached through the "bridges of God" (people representing unreached groups that were present in reached ones), Winter's presentation focused on those to whom no bridges yet existed. But there was decades of research behind this idea, thanks to J. Waskom Pickett and MacGavran. But my point here is that he could stand on his own two feet with regard to ideas.

However, it was innovation that led to so much of Winter's activity. According to business consultant Jay Galbraith, "Breakthrough innovations often come from the interaction of disciplines...In general champions have learned the knowledge in a discipline but have not accepted the religion." This fits Winter well. His formal education and experiences were cross-disciplinary. He had a BA in civil engineering, an MA in TESOL, and after his PhD in linguistics, anthropology and mathematical statistics, he also received an M.Div. Until his death, he subscribed to a very large variety of magazines, many of them scientific in nature and he read widely. Thus he was able to connect areas of knowledge that were not often connected. As a result of this diversity of training and engineering impulse, innovation came naturally and can be traced throughout his life.

Two examples will suffice. First was the establishment of the US Center for World Mission and, three months later, William Carey International University. While these organizations may look like any other mission agency or university, they are in fact very different. One key difference was the formation of the unique community that stands behind them. The modality-sodality concept was prominent in his mind, and he traveled around the country looking at various models of community. What resulted was missionary members who live in community. His deep respect for the Catholic monastic orders led to a mission agency more similar to those orders than most other agencies today. All our members meet each morning to seek God and His Word together. We all live in the same community within a block or two of the main campus. In this way an idea became an innovation, at least in the Protestant world.

Another example of innovation is the "Perspectives on the World Christian Movement" study program. Even after all these years I've yet to see anything comparable. I am not aware of any other "mobilization by education" program that is as extensive and available all around the world. While the content of the class itself is excellent, those would merely be ideas without the delivery mechanism of the class itself. With one dedicated class coordinator, a Perspectives class can begin almost anywhere. The format of rotating lecturers and a well-designed study guide have made it our flagship program. In the US in 2009, we had over 200 classes with 6,500 new students. To date, in America we have over 80,000 alumni, 2000 trained coordinators and 1800 instructors. In Korea, Perspectives started September 2000. As of 2010 May there have been 173 classes and will have 10,450 graduates by the end of May. At the present time, classes are taking place annually in 15 countries of Latin America, Australia, New Zealand, Nigeria, India, South Africa and UK. It is at various stages of translation in many languages, with the goal being not mere translation but indigenous contribution as well. There have also been many derivatives of the course that make up the "Perspectives Family". Most of these are shorter, more concise versions. Many of the concepts in the Perspectives course are not unique or new to mission thinkers. It is the innovation of the class itself and its unique format that has made the content available for the first time to so many.

2. Missiology must be progressive.

There is a direct correlation between our organizational history and Dr. Winter's missiology. The outlines of this progression of thought are best seen in his article, "12 Frontiers of Perspective", where Winter refers to,

> *some of the major shifts or changes of perspective, each, in a way, a "frontier," that has emerged at least in my own thinking since 1976 when I left my professorship at Fuller Theological Seminary. It is as though my thinking has speeded up since then. You might call these emerging perspectives extensions of vision because it isn't as if we have shifted away from something wrong. We have just had deeper and deeper insights into additional things.*

These twelve frontiers of perspective are:

(1) Unreached Peoples
(2) The Great Commission and Abraham
(3) From the Unfinished Task to the Finishable Task
(4) Failure with the large groups and the off-setting trend to "radical contextualization"
(5) Reverse Contextualization, the Re-contextualization of Our Own Tradition
(6) The Reclaiming of the Gospel of the kingdom
(7) Beyond Christianity
(8) A Different Type of Recruitment
(9) A Trojan Horse?
(10)   Needed: a Revolution in Pastoral Training
(11)   The religion of Science
(12)   The Challenge of the Evil One

As we have tried to interpret Dr. Winter's thought, it seems to some of us that he began asking, "where does the gospel need to go?" After some years of seeing the mission movement respond to the unreached peoples challenge, and observing some of the dynamics taking place, he began asking, "what is the nature of the gospel we are taking there?". Toward the end of his life, due to his thinking and his personal experience with cancer, Winter was increasingly drawn to ideas related to evangelical passivity as a response to evil. Many people, including our own members, wondered why he was moving away from an unreached people emphasis. But in his mind, these ideas weren't unrelated, they simply represented deeper insights into the same reality of kingdoms in conflict.

3. Mobilization must be informed

Winter placed a high value on mission practice that was informed. He employed the phrase, "the amateurization of missions" to describe what he saw happening among American evangelicals. Hendrik Kraemer had used the same phrase many years before. Winter even likened the American short-termer as a "dog in a museum" who sees everything but understands nothing. This conviction led to mobilization that was closely tied to training programs and the beginning of William Carey International University. One of the most significant accomplishments of the Center has been the production of various mission curricula. From kindergarten to PhD, curricula have been written with one common denominator, showing God's purposes in history and calling people to informed service. Here are the curricula to date:

(1) K/12 Together curriculum
(2) Judson curriculum
(3) The Blessing curriculum
(4) Foundations curriculum
(5) Perspectives curriculum
(6) INSIGHT curriculum
(7) World Christian Foundations (WCF) curriculum (used in WCIU MA program)
(8) BA degree completion curriculum

The core of all these curricula is essentially the same. Rooted in mission history, they all strive to inspire and enable informed mission practice. Winter practiced "historical exegesis", believing that an understanding of what God has already done in history was a key to anticipating the future. These curricula are to me the greatest legacy of Dr. Winter, because they preserve his thinking for future generations to ponder. Much of what we do now at both the Center and the University involves running programs that use these curricula.

Beyond the curricula, we produce two magazines, *Mission Frontiers* and the *International Journal of Frontier Missions*, which also focus on informed mission practice. While MF is targeted for a broad audience, IJFM is a scholarly journal. In both cases, the purpose is to stimulate dialogue and critique about various aspects of mission. In recent years, we have wrestled with what has come to be called "insider movements", people coming to living faith in Jesus while remaining in the context of their culture, with all the religious dimensions associated with it. This is without a doubt the most explosive current debate we have sought to promote. Yet these issues must be engaged. Our missiology must constantly be challenged and evaluated. Last but certainly not least, is the work of William Carey Library. One of Dr Winter's first innovations that he started while at Fuller, William Carey Library predates the Center and University. It began as the desire to print many of the fine dissertations being produced at Fuller that would not otherwise be seen by others. Dr. Winter and his daughters ran the operation from his home. Eventually, it expanded beyond dissertations and now includes many titles. Affordability was always a main factor, and WCL remains in my opinion the cheapest place to buy mission books. It is interesting to note that the phone number for WCL is 1-800-MISSION. At one point, a representative from the US government wanted to buy the number. However, we refused to give it up, thus keeping mission for God and not man!

PROSPECT

In this section, I switch my attention to the future. It has now been almost one year since Dr. Winter's death. As I look ahead toward our prospects, this is what I'm seeing.

We seek "collaborative genius"

After ten years of research involving 24,000 people in 24 organizations, a group of three scholars have identified five distinct organizational cultures found in any work environment:

Stage 1: negative tone, individual focus
Stage 2: negative tone, group focus
Stage 3: positive tone, individual focus
Stage 4: positive tone, group focus
Stage 5: collaborative genius

The findings show that 49% of the organizations studied are in stage 3. Here is a description of Stage Three; perhaps it describes your organization as well as mine,

People engage in anything that's going on, with energy and commitment, but when you listen closely, they talk mostly about themselves and focus on appearing smarter and better than others. They think they're focused on team concerns, but their actions show their interest is personal...They rarely bring people together, they resist sharing information except when it's necessary, and they pride themselves on being better informed than others. Winning is all that matters, and winning is personal.

Organizations at this stage are made up of people who are "lone warriors", high achievers individually who feel frustrated by others around them whom they perceive to have less ambition or skill. The authors state,

Professionals usually cap out at Stage Three. Attorneys, accountants, physicians, brokers, salespeople, professors, and even the clergy are evaluated by what they know and do, and these measuring points are the hall marks of Stage Three. "Teams" at this point mean a star and a supporting cast – surgeon and nurses, senior attorney and associates, minister and deacons, professor and TAs.

The avenues from stage three to stage four are either 1) a personal epiphany that you can't do it by yourself, you have to work with others, or 2)working on a project that is bigger than one person can take on. In some cases, the personal epiphany is like a conversion experience, when people see something they have never been able to see before. It often comes when people realize that no matter how hard they work and how much they achieve, they will not be able to attain the success they crave. That kind of success can only come with collaboration.

The key to moving into stage four effectiveness is uniting around common values and a noble cause. In Stage Four, people are more concerned with the values and cause of the organization than their own personal place within it. In some Stage Four companies, titles are left off of business cards. This shift in culture is noted by the language used. Instead of "I" or "me", it becomes "we" and "us". Stage Five, which is the final stage, is a kind of nirvana where people compete not against other organizations but against whatever is standing in the way of their cause.

I would like to apply this at two levels. First, I will apply this to our organization and then I will make some speculative comments about the broader mission movement.

First, our own organization is at Stage Three and we are looking to move it into Stage Four. We have resembled the "star and supporting cast" model. But with our star now gone, we are forced to embrace a different model. Our credibility and our viability are at stake. Some have already suggested that we have little to offer to the mission community with the death of Dr. Winter. We are looking to move from individual genius to a more collaborative genius. We have defined our noble cause as "Nothing less than the presence of a community of faith within every people group on earth, where Jesus transforms lives and societies". I presume that all of you would share that vision. Our mission, which applies to our group of organizations specifically is "to advance insights and initiatives of strategic value that enhance the impact of the mission enterprise". Our values are being a committed mission community, practicing a strategic lifestyle, solution-driven innovation, service and partnership, walking our talk and intergenerational mentoring. In the absence of our great thinker and friend, we have new challenges but also new opportunities. What we need to do now is to adapt and overcome. Only time will tell if we are successful.

Now, I would like to focus on the broader picture, moving beyond our context to that of the entire mission enterprise. Everything I say here is speculative and represents only my "sense" and is not the result of major study or long years of experience. The rule of St. Benedict says that an abbot should pay special attention to the ideas of those under his care, especially those who are younger and are new to the order. For some reason, this perspective of the novice was considered important. As a younger person here, and I do this with much trembling, allow me the grace to share the perspective of a novice.

First, I would suggest that the entire mission enterprise is at Stage Three as well. While we talk about partnership, it is usually a surface partnership that is unwilling to risk personal or organizational standing. 2010 is the year of big conferences. This year is historic for those of us in mission. But will they live up to the expectations we have for them, expectations of genuine partnership and collaboration? All four conferences are commemorating in some way Edinburgh 1910. Yet depending on which lens is used to evaluate that conference, it may not be something we wish to emulate. Has much really changed? Are we bound to the "cautious incrementalism" that has been the modus operandi of these past 100 years? Aren't we doing the very same things that were done over the last century? It is telling that the Tokyo 2010 conference may well be the first time in history where a major, global gathering of mission leaders and practitioners will include a minority of Westerners. Yet conferences are but a reflection of reality. Is it a symbol of wishful thinking or a true harbinger of things to come? Is it not time for a paradigm-busting change to emerge that will lead to a new trajectory in true partnership and collaboration? Dr. Winter believed that having a Global Network of Mission Structures (GNMS) was key to our future. The whole Tokyo 2010 concept is based on the hope that such a network will be one of the main outcomes of the meeting. In some ways, what happens after the meeting is more significant than what happens during the meeting. The opportunity is here for a level of global partnership that has never before existed. We have national mission networks and regional networks, but as of today, a global network of mission structures only, has been out of our reach. It is interesting to me that while Winter advocated such a global network of mission structures, he also had very realistic expectations about how hard it is for human beings to work together. He recently said that partnership may be the wrong way forward, suggesting instead that we be "good neighbors" to each other. Whether as partners or good neighbors, it seems that a global network of mission structures, apart from the valid, complementary voice of the church structures, would be a good thing for the 21st Century. Such a network can leverage and focus the unique vision of mission structures in new ways. And perhaps such a network can move forward the entire mission enterprise to Stage Four effectiveness.

What I've shared so far in this "Prospect" section is that we at the US Center and William Carey University are seeking "collaborative genius". I've also suggested the same is necessary in the broader mission enterprise. Finally, I'd like to share two thoughts unrelated to this idea of "collaborative genius".

First, I feel that mission historians are too critical of the Western mission movement, by which I refer specifically for context to the missionary endeavors of American and Western Europeans during the 19th and 20th centuries. Pointing out abuses of power is like proving someone has sinned. They have both been with us since the beginning of time. Does anyone really believe that if the tables were turned, if in recent centuries Africa, Asia and Latin America had the capacity to colonize America and Western Europe, that they would have? Of course they would have. Imperialism and colonialism is a human problem, not merely a Western one. A new book has come out from a French intellectual named Pascal Bruckner entitled, "The Tyranny of Guilt: an Essay on Western Masochism". Note the following review of the book from the Princeton University Press website,

> *Fascism, communism, genocide, slavery, racism, imperialism--the West has no shortage of reasons for guilt. And, indeed, since the Holocaust and the end of World War II, Europeans in particular have been consumed by remorse. But Pascal Bruckner argues that guilt has now gone too far. It has become a pathology, and even an obstacle to fighting today's atrocities. Bruckner, one of France's leading writers and public intellectuals, argues that obsessive guilt has obscured important realities. The West has no monopoly on evil, and has destroyed monsters as well as created them--leading in the abolition of slavery, renouncing colonialism, building peaceful and prosperous communities, and establishing rules and institutions that are models for the world. The West should be proud--and ready to defend itself and its values. This is a searing, provocative, and psychologically penetrating account of the crude thought and bad politics that arise from excessive bad conscience.*

Without going into a debate on that quote, I think there is truth to be found there. I have always found David Bosch's reflections on history profoundly true, that there is a sense of inevitability to what has happened in the past. All of us are people of our times, fish swimming in the water in some ways totally unaware of our opinions, attitudes and actions that future generations will find objectionable. It can be easy to find fault with missionary endeavors of the past, be they western or otherwise. But the truth is that even the very best historians can never know what it is really like to walk in the shoes of those who lived in other eras. We should be cautious in our criticisms and careful in our judgments. Judging past endeavors based on present ways of thinking is unfair. Let us instead stand in awe of the incredible zeal, commitment and sacrifice exhibited by so many missionaries of the past, of all nationalities and persuasions. Those whom we criticize helped build the enterprise we are privileged to serve today. Is our level of zeal, commitment and sacrifice as great as theirs? God bless the memory of all those who've gone before us.

Second, I feel that the words "Western" and "non-Western" are no longer valid categories for mission studies. Newer terms such as the "Global South" are equally unhelpful. Such macro-terms only confuse the fact that all of us come from a certain context, a micro-context where the macro-terms are irrelevant and insufficient. With each passing day, globalization makes these categories less and less relevant. While they may be helpful historical markers to describe a reality that once was, I do not think they adequately or helpfully describe today's situation. Others have pointed out the problems related to the phrase "the West". But the problems are equally true of any macro-term. Take the word "Asia" for instance. On the plane coming here I was reading the compendium of the Asian Society of Missiology Bangkok Conference of 2007. In his article "Asian Mission: Towards a Theological Perspective", Dr. Hidalgo Ban Garcia writes,

> *Which Asia? Asia is perhaps the most varied and complicated continent on earth. There is affluent and developed Asia, and there is poor and suffering Asia. There is Islamic Asia, Buddhist Asia, Hindu Asia, and Roman Catholic Asia. There is Dutch, British, or Spanish previously colonized Asia. And there is modern Asia as well as primitive one.*

And I would add that there is a "Western Asia" and a "non-Western Asia". We might also ask, "which Africa"? or "which Latin America"?

One thing we soon learn in mission is that context is everything. We have recently received some serious accusations against us because of our promotion of what have previously been called "insider movements". But the critique refers only to "the insider movement", as if it is monolithic and rigid. The truth is that there are things happening out there that cover the C-scale spectrum. There is no such thing as "the insider movement". But the point is that the choice in mission methodology is based on context. Nobody we talk to would say that an insider approach is valid everywhere. Little makes sense in mission thinking outside of a particular context. Deep missiological thinking requires the use of micro-terms to describe micro-contexts.

Because of my European descent, many of you may perceive me to be a "Western Christian" or even worse, a "product of Christendom". And it may be partly true. But such an evaluation is unfair to me. It does not take into consideration my upbringing in non-Western contexts. I once took special delight in telling an African-American congregation in Pasadena that I was more African than they were. Most of them had never spent a day of their lives in Africa, where I grew up for 8 years of my childhood. And the African-American culture that I've observed has very little in common with the African culture of my youth. I have also met those from supposed non-Western contexts who seem to be more "western" than I. In all of this, I don't want to pretend that there are not major, deep cultural value differences between different parts of the world. I only suggest that if we have to use these macro-terms, we use them sparingly and only as background for more meaningful discussion.

Categorization is part of the legacy of modernism and it can be very helpful. But I fear that it can also divide. The best category I can think of for mission thinkers is "disciple of Jesus" and I hope for a day when we can interact more on that basis than on the basis of which cultural context we were born into, which of course happened without our consent. Being "western" or "non-Western" is largely a political or national designation. It is the dominant lens people use today to understand themselves. But I don't think it is good enough to describe the Kingdom of God. Personally, my allegiance to the Kingdom is much greater than my allegiance to America. I am not a very patriotic person. Therefore, I struggle when I am defined primarily as "western" or "American". This is not my primary identity as a disciple of

Jesus.   Neither is your primary identity that of being "non-Western" or "Korean".   We are all children of God, called to live under the rule of God, in order to fulfill the purposes of God.   I may be naïve, but I hope the day comes when we can gather under this category rather than the western/non-western one.   Our first birth may divide us in many ways, but our second birth unites in ways that are much, much greater. I propose that we see each other more from the standpoint of our second birth than the first.

Conclusion

In conclusion, I'm in agreement with the thoughts already expressed that God is moving in this world and that we are privy to only a small part of what He is doing.   We really don't know what is going on.   We see through a glass dimly.   In 1 Kings 12, when Rehoboam rejects the elders' advice and responds harshly to the people, it says in verse 15, "this turn of events was from the LORD, to fulfill the word the LORD had spoken". God is turning events to fulfill His Word.   He will turn events so that the gospel will be proclaimed to all peoples.   He will do it in His time and in His way. Whatever we do is complementary.   What He does is primary.   May God give us the grace to see what He is doing and participate gladly in it.

PARTNERSHIP IN MISSIONS RESEARCH AND DEVELOPMENT

Retrospect and Prospect of the Ministries of US Center for World Mission & William Carey International University as Research and Leadership Development

Dr. Eun Moo Lee
Asia Missions Association

PILGRIMAGE IN MISSION
OF DR. DAVID J. CHO

Retrospect and Prospect of the Ministries
of US Center for World Mission
& William Carey International University
as Research and Leadership Development

It is my privilege to present the pilgrimage of Dr. David J. Cho in Asian missions and beyond. He is truly the Father of the Korean mission movement. Dr. John T. Seamands, professor of Asbury Theological Seminary, once called Dr. David J. Cho "Mr. Mission". His life was fully concentrated on and dedicated to the calling for Asians and their responsibility in world mission. Dr. Cho is not known only as a mission statesman in Korea, but also as a successful pastor of a local church, and an expert organizer for church administration. He conducted large rallies, like the Billy Graham Crusade Korea in 1973, and other evangelistic gatherings. He took part in church architecture design, and has written a number of books.

In the following section I would like to focus on his vision, efforts, and contributions to his non-Western mission movement.

FIRST PERIOD:
Opening the Eyes of Korean Churches to World Mission

The Korean Church was established, and experienced rapid growth in the midst of political turbulence and unrest during the Japanese occupation for 36 years. The Korean Church started its ministries with a mission mind. Pastor Lee Ki Poong was sent to Jeju Island as a missionary, one of the first seven seminary graduates in 1907 without any supporters. Korea continued to send a few missionaries to China and Japan without any particular mission structure but the Presbyterian Church General Assembly took an active part.

The Prosperity Theology or the message of blessing was the focus at the time due to the survival and prosperity of human beings after the Japanese occupation and the outbreak of the Korean War. In the 1970s, prayer, revival meetings, and church attendance were all intended for the enhancement of one's own blessing, and not for the blessing of others.

However, Dr. David J. Cho saw the potential of Korean churches since they had endured hardship and difficulties during persecution from both the Japanese regime and communist intervention in the Korean peninsula. When he returned from his various school programs in the USA, including Asbury Theological Seminary where he studied Evangelism in 1964, he began implementation of what he had learned in the USA in his own church first. His vision for the potential of Korean churches recognized their many resources and possibilities

He realized his missionary vision to the Korean church with missionary campaigns (called Mission Revival Meetings) in his own church, Hooam Presbyterian Church, in 1962, which became the birthplace of Korean mission. Many young people attended this type of revival meeting, which was uncommon at the time. People began to realize that the purpose of the local church was to bring souls who are in darkness into the Kingdom, which is the fundamental purpose of the Church's existence.

While sharing mission with others and recruiting resources, both manpower and financial power, he began his mission enterprise by educating and training people. The

International School of Mission (ISM), which was the first official training program for cross-cultural ministries was started in Korea in 1963.

In1968, he formed the first official mission agency in Korea called KEIMA (Korea Evangelistic Inter-Mission Association), which served as an interdenominational agency to reach the world with the gospel of Jesus Christ. This mission agency covered the area of rural mission, literature mission, and foreign mission, and later merged and focused only on foreign mission, at which time the name was changed to KIM (Korea International Mission). This mission agency sent its first missionary Yoon, Do Huck to Hong Kong, and then Shin, Hong Shik to Thailand. Later the mission agency changed once again, and was handed over to a younger generation of mission partners and was called Global Partners, which currently has 266 missionaries serving in 36 countries. Thousands of missionaries were trained under Dr. Cho and served in various mission organizations, particularly GMS (Global Mission Society) which belongs to the Hap-Dong Presbyterian Church, the largest mission agency in Korea with over 2,000 missionaries.

Dr. Cho played a key role in refocusing the Korean Church's outlook to the world, and its responsibility to the world in view of the world mission enterprise. This mission movement caused Korean churches to grow in terms of spiritual maturity and calling.

When Dr. David J. Cho was chairman of the preparatory committee for the Billy Graham Crusade in 1973, the number of Korean churches was over 6 million. Currently there are 10 million Christians in Korea even after a period of decline, and still Korean churches are strong in missions and contribute to the nation as well as the world in leadership and ministry development around the globe.

SECOND PERIOD:
The Emergence of Asian Churches to World Mission

The All Asia Mission Consultation held in 1973, was the first consultation with a mission theme in Asia. Dr. David J. Cho travelled to twelve different Asian countries in 1971 for the purpose of exploring the possibility of bringing outstanding Asian mission leaders together. He and others finally reached a consensus to launch a networking that became the All Asia Mission Consultation held with 26 Asian mission leaders from thirteen Asian countries and four western missiologists. Dr. David J. Cho served as chairperson at the third meeting of the Preparatory Consultation in Lausanne Congress in 1974. He was a plenary speaker on mission strategy at the congress.

In 1975, after two years of this Consultation he conducted and formed the Asia Missions Association (AMA), an official association for all Asian churches and mission agencies. There were a number of mission leaders who participated in this event including Dr. Philip Teng (Hong Kong), Dr. Han Kyung Jik, Rev. Kang Sin Myung (both Korean), Dr. Akira Hatori (Japan), Dr. Chandu Ray (Singapore), Dr. G. D. James (Malaysia), Dr. Petros Octavianus (Indonesia), and representatives from thirteen countries in Asia. AMA affirmed the Seoul Declaration on Christian Mission which is a historic declaration confirming a joint evangelistic work as Asians for Asians and beyond.

The AMA Conferences have been conducted in several countries such as Korea (1975, 1982), Singapore (1978), USA(1986), Japan (1991, 1997), Indonesia (2000), Russia (2003), and Turkey (2006). The next convention will be held in Jakarta, Indonesia in 2010 with a dedication ceremony of a sanctuary in the largest church building that can hold more than 10,000 people. Dr. Jacob Nahuway, the Chairman of AMA, and an alumnus of the East-West Center for Research and Development, is the pastor of this church, the Mawar Saron Church in Jakarta.

At the time when mission training was a new thing,

the Church considered theological training as sufficient to be a missionary. That thought remained until Dr. Cho opened a training program called the Summer Institute of World Mission (SIWM) in 1973. World renown mission scholars and leaders such as Dr. Donald McGavran (Fuller), Dr. Arthur Glasser (Fuller), Dr. Ralph Winter (Fuller), Dr. Peter Wagner (Fuller), Dr. George Peters (Dallas), Dr.Edwin Frizen (IFMA), Dr. Clyde Taylor (EFMA), Dr. Waldron Scott (WEF), and Horace Williamson (WEC) were invited for the purpose of teaching the goal of cooperation. They were the first trainers at the Summer Institute of World Mission, which was a short-term summer training program. The SIWM continues with many western scholars that desire to teach in this program including Dr. Don Blue (Dallas), Dr. Wilber Norton, James Engel (both Wheaton College), Dale Kitezman (William Carey), Donald Smith (Western), and Samuel Kim, Jae Ok Chun, Myung H. Kim, Eun Moo Lee and many more. SIWM produced more than 1,000 missionaries and mission partner churches in Korea, and some outstanding mission centered church pastors such as Hong, Jung Gil, and Ha, Yong Cho.

The East West Center for Missions Research and Development was launched with the purpose of training Asians for missions. A number of students from Asia and Oceania were invited to study in an MA program in Korea, and upon completion were sent back to their own countries to serve in mission as leaders. Some of them established missional churches such as Mawar Saron Church with around 10,000 members, some became mission leaders, and others became missionaries. The Pauline House is a facility to train full-time Korean missionaries, and currently GMS uses the premises for their denominational missionary training program.

THIRD PERIOD:
Third World to World Mission

TWMA (Third World Missions Association) is a mission cooperative organization from the Third World, which was previously considered a mission field. Third World partners join the cooperative work of networking where necessary for effective ministry development. This was a new era of mission cooperation since the non-western Christian population had exceeded the Western Christian population. This mission movement has helped churches from dependency to inter-dependency and finally independency. In 1980 Dr. David J. Cho had already recognized the signs of possibility and realized that without two-way mission cooperation world evangelization would be impossible. The numbers of missionaries from the Third World have exceeded that of the Western world. In other words, God has his own program, and when one side declines the other side is raised up. There will always be someone to take up the burden of this unfinished task.

Dr. Cho took up the Challenge to Impossibility. His passion for the unreached in North Korea brought him to that region over 20 times, trying to build a bridge by opening up a religion department in Kim Il Sung University. He taught at Pyung Yang Seminary and distributed Christian literature and over 2,700 Christian books. He contributed to opening up the way for visiting North Korean politicians to the USA, and made possible the visits of Billy Graham to Pyung Yang for peace negotiations in 1992, and then Jimmy Carter in 1994. The time for sowing is now, but the harvest will come in God's perfect time.

Dr. Cho's latest mission was to Russia. He believes that mission should not be in theory, but in action. Once Dr. Philip Teng stressed mission in his own theological seminary in Hong Kong, and dedicated himself to serve in Kalimantan, Indonesia for a year in 1977, Dr. Cho also went to Russia as a missionary at the age of 78 years old from 2000 to 2003. He taught for two years in the Russian Military Theological Institute, Moscow, Russia. In the final stage of his ministry in Russia he conducted the Asia Missions Association convention in Moscow in 2003.

HIS DISTINCTIVENESS OF MISSIONS

As a visionary for missions

He was a missionary pioneer just as William Carey who established the London Missionary Society, an official mission agency that produced many missionaries and brought mission into the right course. Dr. David J. Cho predicted that Korean churches can produce 10,000 cross-cultural missionaries by the year 2000, even though no one concurred with him in this estimation. Presently there are 130 mission agencies in Korea which have sent 20,500 missionaries to 170 countries. He was a solo mission challenger who stimulated mission in Korea and beyond.

As a futurist for missions

God gave him a futuristic mind as a pioneer in the early stages of Korean church history to bring the wind of mission to Korean churches. As observed, the training program for missionaries was a new thing for Korean churches at the time. As mentioned, he began a mission training program when the Korean churches were ignorant of such methods. He has always led and pioneered ideas for the advancement of missions in regards to training, administration, strategy, and networking for international cooperation.

As he established the identity of Asian missions

His idea for the Asian identity is to encourage Asians in their responsibility to global mission and to help decrease dependency from Western churches in terms of resources. If Western domination of mission continued then people in the Third World would no longer take this great task from them. By the grace of God this great task has been taken up by Third World churches, and the scholars from Asia must seriously consider their way of missiology and strategic development in the future.

As an administrator of missions

A right concept of mission is necessary in order to send the right people to the right place in the right way. From the beginning of the mission enterprise there was agreement of cooperation between the sending and receiving mission agency. Working with the Church of Christ in Thailand, Indonesian Missionary Fellowship, and Asia Evangelistic Fellowship are examples of good cooperative effort conducted by Dr. Cho.

As a missionary trainer

Those who took part in the Pauline House wartime training program have been successfully working around the world. That training style is a timeless and should be maintained. Unfortunately, the ways of Dr. David J. Cho are not well accepted by many of the missionaries of today who seek easy ways of preparation for work on the mission field. Dr. David Cho believes that we have to learn from the Apostolic model of the missionary enterprise, a timeless example of the principle of missions. Mission, the Apostolic Way, was the theme for the AMA Ephesus conference in 2006.

In conclusion I would like to quote the words of General Douglas MacArthur, a hero of the Korean War, who in his speech at the capital on April 19, 1951, said that "Old soldiers never die, they just fade out." Dr. David J. Cho, God has commanded you to share your last drops of perspiration and tears, and now, your passion and spirit for world mission remains forever in our hearts. Thank you very much.

THE EAST-WEST CENTER FOR MISSIONS RESEARCH & DEVELOPMENT

CHRISTIAN LEADERSHIP
ASIA MISSIONS ASSOCIATION
EAST-WEST CENTER
1968
MISSIONS RESEARCH & DEVELOPMENT

PAULINE HOUSE

東西宣教研究開發院
EAST-WEST CENTER FOR MISSIONS

THE EAST-WEST CENTER FOR MISSIONS RESEARCH & DEVELOPMENT

HISTORY

The leaders of churches and missions from fourteen Asian countries have joined to form the Asia Missions Association. At a consultation in Seoul in 1973, they entrusted to Korea International Mission to establish a center of missions research and training in Seoul.

To provide the finest training possible, benefiting from the experience of generations of Western missions, the Korea International Mission planned to establish the East-West Center for Missions Research and Development in Korea.

The Rev. David J. Cho, who had served as the Executive Director of the Consultation, was subsequently appointed by the Continuation Committee as its Secretary-Treasurer. He set a goal of training at least 10,000 Asian missionaries at the Center by the year 2000 A.D.

He took an initiative step of establishing the Summer Institute of World Mission in Seoul, right after the All-Asia Mission Consultation Seoul '73 was held. The Institute was attempted as an experimental project of the permanent East-West Center for Missions Research and Development which was established as a project of the Asia Missions Association. There was no missionary training institute in Asia before this Institute was established.

Since 1973, more than 2,000 candidates and local pastors received their training at the Center until the year 1999. All of the candidates had already finished their college or seminary training. The candidates came from India, Pakistan, Indonesia, Malaysia, Philippines, Thailand, Singapore, Hong Kong as well as from Korea.

The churches in the East were paving the highways to succeed the unfinished task of the world mission from the West. The project for the task of missions research and training has been steadily materialized.

In 1979, the landbreaking service was observed and the campus of the Center was constructed and named as PAULINE HOUSE.

In 1999, the Founder, Dr. David J. Cho, retired and the Pauline House was transferred to GMS (Global Mission Society).

In 2004, a group of leading senior fellow graduates of the Center formed a new Board of the East-West Center for Missions Research and Development to rehabilitate the Center. Dr. David J. Cho, the Founder of the Center, appointed Dr. Timothy Kiho Park, Professor of Fuller School of Intercultural Studies, as the new President to succeed Dr. David J. Cho's position to take initiation for rehabilitation of the Center. He incorporated the Center to California State and began reshaping the program and raising funds for the Center's rehabilitation activities.

PURPOSE

1. To help available missionary manpower keep pace with the population explosion at a time when the Western missionary force is not increasing.

2. To help prepare the Asian missionary force that will be required when China, North Korea and other communist countries open again, even tentatively, to the Gospel.

3. To train Asian personnel in an Asian program with Asian instructors and concepts.

4. To contribute, by joining in a common effort, to greater maturity in relationship between Christian institutions of the East and the West.

5. To invest the long accumulated Western experience and the results of in-depth studies in training the under-utilized missionary resources of the East.

DISTINCTIVES

Since missiology is a new scientific approach in the study of Christian mission, there are very few scholars and experts available in the Western hemisphere as well as in the Third World churches. However, a few decades ago the churches and academic institutes in the West already developed and established the science of missiology as a field independent from the general fields of theology.

1. According to the cardinal spirit of the East-West Center which stresses equal sharing from both East and West. We would like to invite at least half of the faculties of our institute from the West.

2. The center will establish various courses and degrees in Christian missions. We are not only aiming to train young missionary candidates for their future fields but also to encourage eligible missionaries to carry on their research or graduate degree work.

3. Today, we are facing enormously increasing demands from the unreached world for Asian missionaries.
   However, the missionaries who will carry out the task of propagating the Gospel beyond their own

regions are naturally required to be equipped with various skills and techniques in terms of cross-cultural communication, culture and linguistic specialties. Without this special missiological training in addition to their calling, the modern mission will drift far away from success. Therefore it is an acute and urgent task for the Asian churches to train great forces of missions. The Center has pledged to fulfill this historic task for the Lord's harvest fields.

4. For the first five years (1976-1980), the Center has a plan to train at least 250 candidates; half of these future graduates will be those from various countries of Southeast Asia and other parts of the world. For the second five years (1981-1985), we plan to increase the number of graduates from 500 to 1,000. This double or triple multiplicity of students in our training program will be followed every five years, so that our Institute will reach the goal of 10,000 graduates by the year 2000. If we recast our estimated training program, the increased numbers of graduates every five years until the year 2000 will be as follows:

1976-1980: 250 -400
1981-1985: 500 - 1,000
1986-1990: 1,200 – 1,500
1991-1995: 3,000 – 3,500
1996-2000: 5,000 – 6,000

These estimated numbers were vision and plan for the evangelization of the world before the year 2000.

THE DAVID CHO
MISSIOLOGICAL INSTITUTE

THE DAVID CHO
MISSIOLOGICAL INSTITUTE

The Purpose and Inaugural History

In 2004, a number of Korean mission leaders and followers of Dr. David J. Cho, those who learned missions under his guidance, gathered to commemorate Dr. David J. Cho's 80th birthday, an advocate of third-world missionary movement since 1960. They decided to establish a missiological institute that would advance his creative rationales of world missions to the coming generation. In order to recognize this purpose, the institute was named David Cho Missiological Institute. The bylaw of the institute was then drafted.

On November 19, 2004, the board was formed and Dr. David J. Cho was named as the General Director. Dr. Timothy Kiho Park, a professor of Fuller School of World Mission, was appointed as the Executive Director of the institute. Dr, Chong Koo Park, CEO of the Pastoral Monthly of Korea named as the Director for Planning and Development of the Insitute and World Mission Museum.

In 2009, Ms. Helen Cho succeeded Dr. David J. Cho as the Executive Director of the Institute

Responsible Body

The Board of Directors of the DCMI is the responsible body for deciding, controlling, and organizing the institute's operation and activities, as well as setting the standards for achieving goals. There are no more than 24 members on the Operation Board.

Beliefs and Confessions

The Bible is the perfectly inspired word of God, written accurately without error and preserved to instruct the righteousness, faith, and action. This word of God as well as the common confession of the Apostolic faith and the Westminster Confession of Faith are the foundation of the work of the institute.

Finance

The institute relies substantially on the membership fees of supporting organizations and donations of individual Christians, Christian organizations, and private foundations. The institute does not accept any support or aid from governments or politically related entities.